Recipe Round-up

Acknowledgements

This book features recipes
taken from the Dairy Diaries
published between 1982 and 1985,
together with several others
selected from the
Milk Marketing Board archives.

Designed by AMBA Designs

Edited by Sheelagh Donovan

Production John Vanner

Printed by Jarrold Printing, Norwich.

© The Milk Marketing Board 1993.

Recipe Round-up

A SELECTION OF
POPULAR RECIPES FROM PAST
DAIRY DIARIES

Recipe Notes

- 1 -
Follow metric or imperial measurements in
the recipe. Do not mix the two.

- 2 -
When measuring milk, can sizes, etc.
exact measurements have been given.
e.g. 568 ml (1 pint)

- 3 -
All spoon measures are level.
tsp = teaspoon
tbsp = tablespoon

- 4 -
Cooking times may vary slightly,
depending on individual ovens.
Use the centre shelf in the oven
unless otherwise stated.

CALORIES

The calorie values for each recipe have been rounded
up or down to the nearest 5 calories.
'Milk' in the recipes has been calculated as whole milk.
'Cheese' in the recipes has been calculated as full fat
unless otherwise stated.

Ⓕ

This symbol indicates the recipe is suitable for freezing.
Some recipes e.g. those with crunchy toppings,
have not been given the freezer symbol as
the quality of the dish when reheated,
will not match that of the freshly prepared dish.
You may choose to freeze these dishes.

✳ EGGS

The Department of Health advises
that the general public should avoid eating raw eggs
or uncooked food/recipes made from them.

There is a pasteurised dried egg white powder available
that can be substituted in these recipes. Follow the manufacturers
instructions when reconstituting the powder and make a direct
substitution. Do not be deterred by the
gelatine-like odour when the powder is reconstituted.

Contents

Soups

265 Calories per portion

French Onion Soup SERVES 4

Butter - *40g (1½ oz)*
Onions - *350g (12oz), thinly sliced*
Beef stock - *900ml (1½ pint)*
Salt *and freshly ground* **black pepper**
Dry sherry - *10ml (2 tsp), optional*
French bread - *4 slices, thickly sliced*
Cheddar cheese - *50g (2oz), finely grated*

METHOD

1 Melt butter in a large saucepan. Add onions and fry gently until golden brown.

2 Add stock, season lightly and bring to the boil. Cover and simmer gently for 30 minutes. Add sherry if desired.

3 Pour into 4 individual ovenproof bowls. Float a slice of bread in each bowl, sprinkle the bread with cheese and brown under a hot grill until golden. Serve immediately.

170 Calories per portion (F)

Cream of Broccoli Soup SERVES 6

Spring onions - *12, finely sliced*
Carrots - *2 large, sliced*
Celery - *2 sticks, sliced*
Garlic cloves - *2, crushed*
Bay leaf - *1*
Water - *225ml (8 fl oz)*
Broccoli - *350g (12oz), sliced*
Paprika - *2.5ml (½ tsp)*
Chicken stock - *568ml (1 pint)*
Fresh milk - *450ml (¾ pint)*

Salt *and freshly ground* **black pepper**
Fresh single cream - *150ml (5 fl oz)*
Croûtons - *to serve*

METHOD

1 Place spring onions, carrot, celery, garlic and bay leaf into a large saucepan. Add the water and bring to the boil. Cover and simmer gently for 15-20 minutes or until the vegetables are tender.

2 Remove from the heat then add broccoli, paprika, stock and milk. Season lightly, return to the heat and cook for a further 10 minutes, stirring occasionally.

3 Cool slightly then purée in a food processor or blender until smooth. Stir in most of the cream, saving a little for garnish.

4 Reheat gently. Garnish with fresh cream and croûtons.

75 Calories per portion

Cool Cucumber Soup SERVES 6

Cucumber - *1, grated or finely chopped*
Low fat natural yogurt - *300g (10oz)*
Fresh parsley - *15ml (1 tbsp) chopped*
Fresh chives - *15ml (1 tbsp) chopped*
Garlic clove - *1, crushed*
White wine vinegar - *30ml (2 tbsp)*
Salt *and freshly ground* **black pepper**
Fresh milk - *300ml (½ pint)*
Fresh single cream - *15ml (1 tbsp), to serve*
Parsley - *chopped, to serve*

METHOD

1 Place cucumber in a large bowl and stir in the yogurt, parsley, chives, garlic and wine vinegar. Season to taste.

2 Place bowl in a refrigerator for several hours to chill thoroughly.

3 Just before serving, stir in the milk, check seasoning and garnish with fresh cream and parsley.

N.B. For a richer soup, use Greek style yogurt.

200 Calories per portion Ⓕ

Cream of Mushroom Soup SERVES 3

Chicken stock - *300ml (½ pint)*
Fresh milk - *300ml (½ pint)*
Butter - *25g (1oz)*
Plain flour - *25g (1oz)*
Salt *and freshly ground* **black pepper**
Fresh parsley - *15ml (1 tbsp) chopped*
Button mushrooms - *100g (4oz) finely chopped*

Lemon juice - *15ml (1 tbsp)*
Fresh single cream - *30ml (2 tbsp)*
Parsley - *chopped, to serve*

METHOD

1 Place stock, milk, butter and flour in a saucepan, heat stirring continuously until the mixture thickens and boils. Season lightly, add parsley and mushrooms, cover and simmer gently for 10 minutes.

2 Remove from the heat, stir in lemon juice and cream. Serve garnished with chopped parsley.

230 Calories per portion Ⓕ

Cream of Chestnut Soup

SERVES 6

Chestnuts - *450g (1lb)*
Onion - *100g (4oz) chopped*
Butter - *25g (1oz)*
Chicken stock - *568ml (1 pint)*
Salt *and freshly ground* **black pepper**
Fresh milk - *300ml (½ pint)*
Fresh single cream - *150ml (5 fl oz)*
Parsley - *chopped, to serve*

METHOD

1 Make a small slit near the pointed end of the chestnuts.
Place in a basin, cover with boiling water and leave for
5 minutes. Remove chestnuts from the water one at a time
and peel off the outer and inner skin while still warm.
Be careful not to burn your fingers when removing the skin!

2 Place peeled chestnuts in a saucepan with the onion, butter
and stock. Season lightly, cover and simmer gently for
45 minutes. Cool slightly, then purée in a food processor
or blender until smooth.

3 Return to a clean saucepan, add
milk and cream, check seasoning
and reheat gently.
Serve garnished with parsley.

180 Calories per portion Ⓕ

Carrot & Orange Soup

SERVES 4

Onion - *1, sliced*
Carrots - *450g (1lb) sliced*
Bay leaf - *1*
Fresh milk - *300ml (½ pint)*
Chicken stock - *300ml (½ pint)*
Salt *and freshly ground* **black pepper**
Orange - *grated rind and juice of 1*
Fresh single cream - *150ml (5 fl oz)*

METHOD

1 Place onion, carrot, bay leaf, milk and stock in a large
saucepan. Season lightly, cover and bring to the boil.
Simmer gently for 20 minutes, until the carrot is tender.

2 Remove the bay leaf and cool slightly. Purée in a food
processor or blender until smooth. Return to a clean saucepan,
stir in the orange rind and juice and reheat gently. Stir in the
fresh cream. Serve hot.
Alternatively, cool quickly then refrigerate for several
hours and serve chilled.

N.B. If the soup is to be made in advance,
do not add orange juice and rind until
reheating or the soup will curdle
on standing.

365 Calories per portion ⓕ

Turkey Chowder SERVES 4

Streaky bacon - *100g (4oz) chopped*
Onion - *1 small, chopped*
Carrots - *2 medium, sliced*
Potatoes - *3 medium, diced*
Turkey stock - *568ml (1 pint)*
Salt *and freshly ground* **black pepper**
Cooked turkey meat - *175g (6oz) chopped*
Frozen peas - *100g (4oz)*
Cornflour - *15g (½ oz)*
Fresh milk - *300ml (½ pint)*
Fresh parsley - *chopped, to serve*

METHOD

1 Fry bacon in a large saucepan over a medium heat until fat
begins to run. Add onion and carrots and fry gently for
5 minutes. Add potatoes and stock and season lightly. Bring
to the boil, cover and simmer gently for 15 minutes.
Add turkey and peas and simmer a further 5 minutes.
Remove from the heat.
2 Blend cornflour with a little milk in a jug, add the remaining
milk. Pour the mixture into the soup, stirring all the time.
Bring to the boil, stirring gently and simmer for 2 minutes.
Serve garnished with parsley.

150 Calories per portion ⓕ

Leek & Celery Soup SERVES 6

Butter - *25g (1oz)*
Leeks - *350g (12oz) sliced*
Celery - *4 sticks, sliced*
Onion - *1 large, sliced*
Salt *and freshly ground* **black pepper**
Chicken stock - *568ml (1 pint)*
Fresh milk - *300ml (½ pint)*
Fresh parsley - *25g (1oz) chopped*
Fresh single cream - *150ml (5 fl oz)*

METHOD

1 Melt the butter in a large saucepan, add the leeks,
celery, onion and season lightly. Cook over a medium heat
until the onion is tender. Add the stock, cover and simmer
for 1 hour. Stir in the milk, then purée in a food processor
or blender until smooth.
2 Return to a clean saucepan and reheat gently.
Check seasoning, then stir in most of the
parsley and the fresh cream.
Serve garnished with
remaining
parsley.

210 Calories per portion Ⓕ

Butter Bean Soup SERVES 4

Butter beans - *100g (4oz)*
Water - *568ml (1 pint)*
Celery - *2 sticks, chopped*
Carrots - *2 large, sliced*
Leeks - *2, sliced*
Onion - *1 large, sliced*
Dried thyme - *pinch*
Cayenne pepper - *pinch*
Bayleaf - *1*

Salt - *5ml (1 tsp)*
Black pepper - *2.5ml (½ tsp) freshly ground*
Fresh milk - *300ml (½ pint)*
Greek style yogurt - *60ml (4 tbsp)*
Fresh parsley - *chopped, to serve*
Croûtons - *to serve*

METHOD

1 Place beans in a saucepan, cover with water and bring to the boil.
Pour into a bowl, cover and leave overnight. Drain.

2 Place beans in a saucepan, add measured water, bring to the boil
then add celery, carrot, leeks, onion, thyme, cayenne and bay leaf.
Season. Cover, bring to the boil and simmer gently for 45 minutes
or until the beans are tender. Cool slightly.

3 Purée in a food processor or blender until smooth.
Return to a clean saucepan, add milk and yogurt and reheat
gently without boiling. Serve with parsley and croûtons.

290 Calories per portion Ⓕ

Smoked Fish Soup SERVES 4

Onion - *1 medium, chopped*
Potatoes - *175g (6oz) diced*
Carrots - *100g (4oz) grated*
Celery - *3 sticks, chopped*
Butter - *25g (1oz)*
Fish/chicken stock - *150ml (¼ pint)*
Smoked haddock - *350g (12oz) skinned, cut in chunks*
Fresh milk - *300ml (½ pint)*
Cornflour - *30ml (2 tbsp)*
Pepper - *freshly ground*
Fresh single cream - *75ml (2½ fl oz)*
Chopped parsley - *to garnish*

METHOD

1 Fry the onion, potatoes, carrot and celery in the
butter. Add the stock. Simmer for 10 minutes until
the potatoes are tender.

2 Add the fish and most of the milk. Bring gently to
the boil and simmer for 3-5 minutes.

3 Blend the cornflour with remaining milk and pour
into the soup, stirring all the time. Bring to the boil.

4 Remove from the heat, season with pepper, stir
in the cream and serve garnished with parsley.

258 Calories per portion Ⓕ

Vegetable Chowder SERVES 4

Wholemeal macaroni - *100g (4oz)*
Onion - *1 medium, sliced*
Carrots - *225g (8oz) sliced*
Celery - *3 sticks, sliced*
Butter - *25g (1oz)*
Canned tomatoes - *397g (14oz) can, chopped*
Vegetable/ chicken stock - *300ml (½ pint)*
Bay leaf - *1*
Dried oregano - *5ml (1 tsp)*
Salt *and freshly ground* **black pepper**
Fresh milk - *300ml (½ pint)*
Chopped parsley - *to garnish*

METHOD

1 Cook the macaroni as directed on the packet.

2 Fry the onion, carrots and celery in the butter for 2 minutes.

3 Add the tomatoes, stock, bay leaf and oregano. Season lightly and simmer until vegetables are tender.

4 Stir in the macaroni and milk. Bring gently to the boil. Remove the bay leaf and serve sprinkled with parsley.

---

340 Calories per portion Ⓕ

Sweetcorn & Green Pepper Soup SERVES 4

Butter - *40g (1½ oz)*
Onion - *1, chopped*
Green pepper - *1, deseeded and sliced*
Button mushrooms - *100g (4oz) sliced*
Plain flour - *25g (1oz)*
Chicken stock - *300ml (½ pint)*

Sweetcorn kernels - *225g (8oz)*
Potatoes - *2 medium, chopped*
Salt *and freshly ground* **black pepper**
Fresh milk - *300ml (½ pint)*
Fresh single cream -
  75ml (2½ fl oz)

METHOD

1 Melt butter in a large saucepan and gently fry onion, pepper and mushrooms for 3 minutes.

2 Stir in flour and cook for 2 minutes. Add stock, sweetcorn, potatoes and season lightly.

3 Bring to the boil, add milk and simmer gently for 30 minutes. Stir in cream and reheat gently.

315 Calories per portion Ⓕ

Country Pâté SERVES 6

Streaky bacon - *5-6 rashers de-rinded*
Plain flour - *15g (½ oz)*
Butter - *15g (½ oz)*
Fresh milk - *150ml (¼ pint)*
Belly pork - *100g (4oz)*
Pigs liver - *100g (4oz)*
Onion - *25g (1oz)*
Sausage meat - *100g (4oz)*
Garlic clove - *1 crushed*
Dry sherry or brandy - *30ml (2 tbsp)*
Salt *and freshly ground* **black pepper**
Bay leaf - *1*
Hot toast - *to serve*

METHOD

1 Stretch bacon with the back of a knife and use to line a 450g (1lb) terrine or loaf tin.

2 Place flour, butter and milk in a saucepan, heat stirring continuously until the sauce thickens, boils and is smooth.

3 Mince the pork, liver, onion and sausagemeat together twice and add to the sauce. Stir in the garlic and sherry or brandy. Season.

4 Turn the mixture into the lined tin, smooth the surface and top with the bay leaf. Cover with foil or a lid and stand in a roasting tin half filled with boiling water. Cook at 180°C (350°F), mark 4 for 1 hour.

5 Allow the pâté to cool slightly then place a weight on the top and refrigerate overnight to allow the flavours to develop. Turn out and serve with slices of hot toast.

255 Calories per portion

Stilton Mousse SERVES 6

Gelatine - *11g sachet*
Chicken stock cube - *1*
Stilton cheese - *225g (8oz)*
Fresh milk - *150ml (¼ pint)*

Walnuts - *50g (2oz) chopped*
Egg whites* - *2 (size 3)*
Watercress - *to serve*
Cucumber - *sliced*
*See page 2.

METHOD

1 Sprinkle gelatine over a little warm water in a basin and leave to soak. Place the basin over a pan of simmering water and stir until dissolved. Make up to 300ml (½ pint) with very hot water. Crumble in the stock cube, stir until dissolved. Leave to cool.

2 Mash Stilton cheese in a large basin, blend in the cooled gelatine, followed by the milk and walnuts.

3 When the cheese mixture is beginning to set, whisk the egg whites until stiff and fold one tablespoonful gently into the cheese mixture. When well blended, fold in the remaining egg white.

4 Turn into a wetted 900ml (1½ pint) ring mould and chill until firm. To serve, turn onto a serving plate and garnish with watercress and sliced cucumber.

470 Calories per portion

Hot Cheese Stuffed Eggs SERVES 4

Hard boiled eggs - *4 (size 3)*
Butter - *50g (2oz) softened*
English Cheddar - *75g (3oz) grated*
Garlic clove - *1 crushed*
Fresh milk - *15ml (1 tbsp)*
Salt *and freshly ground* **black pepper**

Button mushrooms - *8, cooked*
Watercress - *to serve*

CHEESE SAUCE:
Butter - *15g (½ oz)*
Plain flour - *25g (1oz)*
Fresh milk - *300ml (½ pint)*
English Cheddar - *50g (2oz) grated*
Salt and cayenne pepper

METHOD

1 Cut the hard boiled eggs in half and remove the yolks. Mash yolks and blend in the butter, 50g/2oz of the grated cheese, garlic and milk. Season lightly.

2 Divide mixture between the halved egg whites and place around the edge of a lightly greased shallow ovenproof dish.

3 To make the cheese sauce, place the butter, flour and milk in a saucepan, heat stirring continuously until the sauce thickens, boils and is smooth. Cook for one minute. Remove from the heat, add grated cheese and stir off the heat until it has melted. Season lightly.

4 Pour sauce over the stuffed eggs and sprinkle with remaining cheese. Brown under a hot grill, serve garnished with mushrooms and watercress.

---

620 Calories in the total mixture

Chicken Savouries MAKES 16

Fresh milk - *150ml (¼ pint)*
Butter - *15g (½ oz)*
Plain flour - *15g (½ oz)*
Natural yogurt - *150g (5oz)*
Cucumber - *½, chopped*
Pickled gherkins - *50g (2oz) chopped*
Celery - *2 sticks chopped*
Cooked chicken - *175g (6oz) chopped*
Salt *and freshly ground* **black pepper**
Savoury biscuits - *to serve*
Parsley - *chopped, to serve*

METHOD

1 Place milk, butter and flour in a saucepan. Heat stirring continuously until the sauce thickens, boils and is smooth. Cook for a minute. Allow to cool.

2 Blend sauce and yogurt together and add cucumber, gherkins, celery and chicken. Season lightly and mix well. Chill for several hours and serve on biscuits, garnished with parsley.

Starters

510 Calories per portion

Avocado Hot Cheese Special

SERVES 4

Fresh milk - *450ml (¾ pint)*
Plain flour - *50g (2oz)*
Butter - *40g (1½ oz)*
Mustard - *5ml (1 tsp) ready made*
English Cheddar cheese - *175g (6oz) grated*
Salt *and freshly ground* **black pepper**
Avocado - *2 skinned and chopped*
Fresh parsley and croûtons - *to garnish*

METHOD

1 Place milk, flour and butter in a saucepan, heat stirring continuously until the sauce thickens, boils and is smooth. Cook for one minute.

2 Remove from the heat and add mustard, 100g (4oz) cheese and season lightly. Gently fold in the avocado and spoon into individual ovenproof dishes. Sprinkle with the remaining cheese and grill until bubbling and golden. Garnish with parsley and croûtons.

---

190 Calories per portion

Smoked Mackerel Mousse

SERVES 6

Plain flour - *15g (½ oz)*
Butter - *15g (½ oz)*
Fresh milk - *150ml (¼ pint)*
Smoked mackerel fillets - *225g (8oz)*
Creamed horseradish sauce - *15ml (1 tbsp)*
Fresh soured cream - *150ml (5 fl oz)*

Black pepper - *freshly ground*
Gelatine - *5ml (1 tsp)*
Lemon juice - *30ml (2 tbsp)*
Egg white* - *1 (size 3)*
Lemon slices, radish,
Parsley - *to garnish*
*See page 2.

METHOD

1 Place the flour, butter and milk in a saucepan, heat stirring continuously until the sauce thickens, boils and is smooth. Cook for one minute. Cool. (This produces a thick sauce.)

2 Remove the skin and any bones from the mackerel and mash the flesh well. Blend in the horseradish sauce, soured cream and cooled sauce. Season with pepper.

3 Sprinkle gelatine over the lemon juice in a small bowl. Stir well. Place the bowl over a pan of simmering water, stir until dissolved. Gradually pour into the fish mixture, stirring continuously until well blended.

4 Whisk egg white until stiff. Gently fold one tablespoon into the fish mixture, followed by the remaining egg white. Stir gently until well blended.

5 Spoon into 6 ramekin dishes and chill for 3-4 hours. Serve garnished with lemon slices, radish roses and parsley.

215 Calories per portion Ⓕ

Chicken Liver Pâté SERVES 6

Butter - *25g (1oz)*
Onion - *1 small, finely chopped*
Garlic clove - *1 crushed*
Chicken livers - *450g (1lb) trimmed and chopped*
Bay leaves - *2*
Dried thyme - *2.5ml (½ tsp)*
Salt *and freshly ground* **black pepper**
Brandy - *30ml (2 tbsp)*
Fresh double cream - *75ml (5 tbsp)*
Lemon - *2 slices, to garnish*
Bay leaves - *2 to garnish*

METHOD

1 Melt the butter and gently fry the onion and garlic. Add livers, bay leaves and thyme and season lightly. Cover and simmer gently for about 10 minutes or until the livers are tender. Remove bay leaves and add the brandy.

2 Cool slightly, transfer to a food processor or blender and work until smooth. Stir in the cream and check seasoning.

3 Pour into a large serving dish and chill for 2-3 hours. Serve garnished with lemon slices and bay leaves.

175 Calories per portion

Savoury Stuffed Eggs SERVES 4

Hard boiled eggs - *4 (size 3)*
Cottage cheese - *25g (1 oz)*
English Cheddar cheese - *25g (1oz) grated*
Fresh single cream - *45ml (3 tbsp)*
Salted peanuts - *25g (1oz) crushed*
Pepper - *freshly ground*
Lettuce - *to serve*
Paprika - *to garnish*

METHOD

1 Cut the hard boiled eggs in half and remove the yolks. Place yolks, cottage cheese, grated cheese, cream, peanuts and several twists of black pepper in a basin and blend well.

2 Pile or pipe the mixture back into the egg whites, arrange on a bed of lettuce and sprinkle with paprika.

380 Calories per portion Ⓕ

Liver Pâté

Streaky bacon - *225g (8oz) de-rinded*
Lambs liver - *350g (12oz) chopped*
Chicken livers - *225g (8oz) chopped*
Onion - *1 small, chopped*
Garlic clove - *1 crushed*
Butter - *15g (½ oz)*
Plain flour - *25g (1oz)*
Fresh milk - *300ml (½ pint)*
Mixed herbs - *pinch*
Ground nutmeg - *pinch*
Salt *and freshly ground* **black pepper**
Cucumber - *slices, to garnish*

METHOD

1 Stretch half the bacon rashers with the back of a knife and use to line a 450g (1lb) loaf tin.

2 Roughly chop the remaining bacon and add livers, onion and garlic. Transfer to a processor or liquidiser or mincer and work until smooth.

3 Place butter, flour and milk in a saucepan. Heat stirring continuously until the sauce thickens, boils and is smooth. Cook for one minute. Add herbs, nutmeg and season lightly. Stir into liver mixture.

4 Pour the mixture into the lined tin, smooth the surface and cover with foil. Stand in a roasting tin half filled with boiling water. Cook at 180°C (350°F) mark 4 for 1¼ hours.

5 Allow pâté to cool, remove foil, cover with greaseproof then place a weight on top. Refrigerate overnight, then turn out and serve garnished with cucumber.

180 Calories per portion Ⓕ

Kipper Pâté SERVES 4

Kipper fillets with butter - *175g (6oz) pack*
Lemon juice - *30ml (2 tbsp)*
Butter - *15g (½ oz) softened*
Fresh double cream - *45ml (3 tbsp)*
Black pepper - *freshly ground*
Lemon slices and parsley - *to garnish*
Crispbread - *to serve*

METHOD

1 Cook kippers as directed on the packet. Tip kippers and juices into a basin and remove the skin. Mash with lemon juice and butter.

2 Beat in the cream and add pepper to taste. Pile into a serving dish and chill for several hours.
Serve garnished with lemon and parsley.

300 Calories per portion Ⓕ

Fisherman's Special

SERVES 4

Smoked haddock - *450g (1lb)*
Fresh milk - *300ml (½ pint)*
Plain flour - *25g (1oz)*
Butter - *15g (½ oz)*
Dried mixed herbs - *pinch*
Salt *and freshly ground* **black pepper**
Parsley - *15ml (1 tbsp) chopped*
Frozen peas - *50g (2oz) cooked*
Hardboiled egg - *1 (size 3) chopped*
Potatoes - *450g (1lb) cooked and mashed*
Lemon slices and parsley - *to garnish*

METHOD

1 Poach the fish in milk for about 10 minutes or until tender. Drain, reserving the liquor.

2 Place fish liquor, flour, butter and herbs in a saucepan and heat stirring continuously until the sauce thickens and boils. Season lightly and add parsley, peas, egg and flaked fish. Divide between 4 individual ovenproof dishes, pipe mashed potatoes around the edge and grill until golden. Serve garnished with lemon and parsley.

300 Calories per portion Ⓕ

Salmon Mousse

SERVES 6

Fresh milk - *300ml (½ pint)*
Plain flour - *25g (1oz)*
Butter - *15g (½ oz)*
Salt *and freshly ground* **black pepper**
Lemon - *1, juice only*
Canned salmon - *439g (15½ oz) can, drained*
Tomato purée - *30ml (2 tbsp)*
Gelatine - *11g sachet*
Fresh double cream - *150ml (5 fl oz) lightly whipped*
Egg whites* - *2 (size 3)*
Cucumber, lemon, capers, olives - *to garnish*
*See page 2.

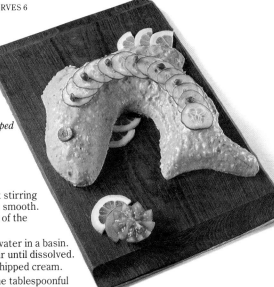

METHOD

1 Place milk, flour and butter in a saucepan, heat stirring continuously until the sauce thickens, boils and is smooth. Cook for one minute, season lightly and add juice of the lemon. Stir in flaked salmon and tomato purée.

2 Sprinkle gelatine over 4 tablespoons of warm water in a basin. Place basin over a pan of simmering water and stir until dissolved. Blend into the salmon mixture, followed by the whipped cream.

3 Stiffly whisk the egg whites then gently fold one tablespoonful into the salmon mixture. Lightly fold in the remainder. Pour into a lightly greased mould and chill until set. Serve decorated with sliced cucumber, lemon, capers and olives.

Calories per dip

Christmas Cocktails

PÂTÉ DIP   *810 Calories*
Liver sausage – *100g (4oz)* Mashed with
Cream cheese – *75g (3oz)* and
Worcestershire Sauce – *15ml (1 tbsp)*
Stir in sufficient
Single cream to give a soft consistency.
Season with
Black pepper – *freshly ground*
Chill.
Turn into a serving dish and serve with
Melba toast.

AVOCADO DIP   *435 Calories*
Smoothly mash the flesh of
1 large avocado in a basin then blend in
Low fat fromage frais – *75g (3oz)*
Single cream – *45ml (3 tbsp)* and
Wine vinegar – *10ml (2 tsp)* Season well with
Black pepper – *freshy ground*. Add
Crushed garlic to own preference.
Chill. Turn into a serving dish and
serve with fingers of
Crisp vegetables.

RED HORSE DIP   *510 Calories*
Redcurrant jelly – *30ml (2 tbsp)* Mixed with
Horseradish sauce – *30ml (2 tbsp)*
Mashed cottage cheese – *100g (4oz)*
Beetroot – *100g (4oz) cooked, finely grated*
and
Soured cream – *150ml (5 fl oz)*.
Season and chill.
Turn into a serving dish.
Serve with
Baby sausages or
Meatballs on sticks.

534 Calories per portion

Seafood Vol au Vent   SERVES 2

Frozen puff pastry - *half a 215g (7½ oz) packet, thawed*
Egg - *1, for brushing pastry*
Fresh milk - *300ml (½ pint)*
Cod or Haddock fillet - *225g (8oz)*
Bay leaf - *1*
Onion - *1 small, sliced*

Butter - *15g (½ oz)*
Plain flour - *25g (1oz)*
Salt *and freshly ground* **black pepper**
Prawns - *50g (2oz)*
Whole prawns - *2 for garnish*

METHOD

1   Roll out pastry into 2 oblongs, 10 x 15cm (4 x 6 inches) each.
Cut each into a heart shape. With a sharp knife, mark another heart
2cm (¾ inch) inside each heart, cutting about halfway through the
pastry. This will form the lid. Place on a wetted baking sheet,
brush with beaten egg and bake at 220°C (425°F), mark 7
for 20 minutes or until risen and golden. Remove the lids
and scoop out any soft pastry. Switch off the oven and
return hearts for about 5 minutes to dry out.

2   Place fish, milk, bay leaf and onion into a saucepan
and simmer for 15 minutes until fish flakes easily.
Drain, reserving fish and liquor.

3   Place liquor, butter and flour in a saucepan,
heat stirring continuously until the sauce thickens,
boils and is smooth. Cook for one minute, season
lightly and add flaked fish and prawns.
Pile into the cases, place lids on top and garnish with whole prawns.

310 Calories per portion Ⓕ

Cod Scallops   SERVES 4

Fresh milk - *300ml (½ pint)*
Onion - *¼, small*
Black peppercorns - *6*
Frozen cod steaks - *4, thawed*
Lemon juice - *30ml (2 tbsp)*
Salt *and freshly ground* **black pepper**
Button mushrooms - *75g (3oz) sliced*
Tomatoes - *100g (4oz), skinned and sliced*
Butter - *15g (½ oz)*
Plain flour - *25g (1oz)*
Leicester cheese - *100g (4oz) grated*
Fresh breadcrumbs - *25g (1oz)*
Tomato and parsley - *to garnish*

METHOD

1 Place milk, onion and peppercorns in a saucepan. Heat until almost boiling, cover and infuse for 15 minutes.

2 Cut fish into strips and arrange in 4 lightly greased ovenproof dishes. Sprinkle with lemon juice, season lightly and cover with sliced mushrooms and tomatoes.

3 Place strained milk in a saucepan with the butter and flour, heat stirring continuously until the sauce thickens, boils and is smooth. Cook for one minute then check seasoning.

4 Pour sauce over fish, sprinkle with a mixture of cheese and breadcrumbs and bake at 180°C (350°F) mark 4 for 25 minutes.
Serve garnished with tomato and parsley.

---

680 Calories in total dip Ⓕ

Stilton Dip   SERVES 4-6

Stilton cheese - *75g (3oz)*
Natural yogurt - *150g (5oz) low fat*
Fresh double cream - *75ml (5 tbsp) lightly whipped*
Parsley - *10ml (2 tsp) chopped*
Black pepper - *freshly ground*
Savoury biscuits and raw vegetables - *to serve*

METHOD

1 Mash the Stilton and blend in the yogurt, followed by the whipped cream and parsley. Season lightly and chill for several hours.

2 Serve in a bowl, surrounded by a selection of savoury biscuits, raw carrot, celery and cucumber sticks.

345 Calories per portion

Chicken & Mushroom Vol au Vents SERVES 4

Frozen puff pastry - *215g (7½ oz) packet, thawed*
Egg - *1, for brushing pastry*
Button mushrooms - *50g (2oz) chopped*
Butter - *15g (½ oz)*
Cooked chicken - *100g (4oz) chopped*
Béchamel sauce - *150ml (¼ pint)*
Lemon juice - *10ml (2 tsp)*

METHOD

1 Roll out pastry to ½ cm (¼ inch) thickness. Cut
into 4 rounds with a 9cm (3½ inch) cutter. Cut part
way through the centre of each round with a 4cm
(1½ inch) cutter. This will form the lid. Place on a
wetted baking sheet, brush with beaten egg and
bake at 220°C (425°F), mark 7 for 10-15 minutes
or until golden and well risen.
Remove the lids and scoop out any soft pastry.
Switch off the oven and return cases for about
5 minutes to dry out.

2 Gently fry the mushrooms in the butter, stir in
the chicken and add to the sauce with the lemon
juice. Reheat until piping hot. Spoon into the pastry
cases, top with lids and serve immediately.

430 Calories per portion

Savoury Croûtes SERVES 4

Egg - *1 (size 3) lightly beaten*
Fresh milk - *150ml (¼ pint)*
Bread - *4 thick slices*
Oil - *for frying*
Streaky bacon - *150g (5oz) chopped*
Onion - *1 medium, thinly sliced*
Button mushrooms - *100g (4oz) sliced*
Tomatoes - *4 small, skinned and chopped*
Fresh or dried mixed herbs - *optional*
Salt *and freshly ground* **black pepper**
English Cheddar cheese - *100g (4oz) sliced*
Watercress - *for garnish*

METHOD

1 Blend the egg and milk. Use to coat both sides
of the bread.

2 Heat a little oil in a frying pan and fry bread until
golden on both sides. Keep warm.

3 Gently fry the bacon until crisp. Drain off excess
fat. Add onions, mushrooms, tomatoes and herbs.
Season lightly. Cook for 5 minutes.

4 Pile the topping onto the croûtes, cover with
slices of cheese and grill until golden and bubbling.
Serve garnished with watercress.

195 Calories per portion

Avocado Cocktail SERVES 4

Ripe avocados - *2 medium*
Lemon juice - *10ml (2 tsp)*
Cottage cheese - *100g (4oz) drained*
Prawns - *50g (2oz)*
Low calorie mayonnaise - *30ml (2 tbsp)*
Tomato purée - *5ml (1 tsp)*
Tabasco sauce - *dash*
Salt *and freshly ground* **black pepper**
Whole prawns - *4 for garnish*
Lemon slices - *for garnish*

METHOD

1 Halve the avocados and remove the stones.
Sprinkle the flesh with lemon juice.

2 Place half an avocado on each of 4 serving
plates.

3 Mix the remaining ingredients together.
Pile into the centre of the avocados.
Serve chilled, garnished with the whole prawns and
lemon.

140 Calories per portion

Stuffed Tomatoes SERVES 4

Beefsteak tomatoes - *4*
English Cheddar cheese - *50g (2oz)*
Cottage cheese - *225g (8oz) drained*
Spring onions - *2 chopped*
Cucumber - *¼, diced*
Ground coriander - *pinch*

METHOD

1 Slice about one third off the top of each tomato
and scoop out the flesh. Drain the flesh,
discarding the juice, core and pips.

2 Combine the chopped flesh with the
remaining ingredients. Season lightly and
refrigerate for 1 hour.

3 Place a tomato shell on each of 4 serving
plates. Divide the filling between them.
Serve chilled.

265 Calories per portion

Oriental Salad SERVES 4

English Mozzarella cheese - *175g (6oz) diced*
Bean sprouts - *100g (4oz) washed and drained*
Radish - *40g (1½ oz) sliced*
White grapes - *50g (2oz) halved and de-pipped*
Chinese leaves - *50g (2oz) finely shredded*
Vinaigrette dressing - *60ml (4 tbsp)*
Radichio leaves - *for serving*

METHOD

1 Toss all the ingredients together
apart from the radichio leaves.

2 Divide the salad between 4 serving
plates and tuck radichio under the
salad as shown in the photograph.
Serve immediately.

290 Calories per portion

Sweet & Savoury Salad SERVES 4

Oranges - *2 medium*
Walnut pieces - *25g (1oz) chopped*
Cheshire cheese - *175g (6oz) cubed*
Dates - *25g (1oz) chopped*
Celery - *2 sticks, chopped*
Fresh soured cream - *60ml (4 tbsp)*
Fresh milk - *15ml (1 tbsp)*
Lettuce - *4 leaves, shredded*

METHOD

1 Finely grate the rind from half one of the oranges
into a basin. Peel the oranges and remove pith and pips.
Chop into bite size pieces, reserving any juice.

2 Add the orange pieces, walnuts, cheese, dates and
celery to the rind in the basin.

3 Blend the soured cream and milk. Stir in any reserved orange
juice and pour over the ingredients in the basin – reserving a little
for serving. Chill.

4 Divide the lettuce between 4 serving dishes and spoon the cocktail
on top. Serve with the remaining dressing drizzled over the surface.

160 Calories per portion

Rosy Pear Salad SERVES 4

Ripe comice pears - *4*
Red skinned apple - *1, cored and chopped*
Cottage cheese - *100g (4oz)*
Lemon - *1, grated rind and juice*
Lancashire cheese - *50g (2oz)*
Streaky bacon - *2 rashers, grilled*

METHOD

1 Halve the pears and remove the cores.

2 Mix the remaining ingredients together and chill for 1 hour.

3 Place each pear half in an individual serving dish and fill the centre with the cheese mixture.
Serve immediately.

225 Calories per portion

Pasta Salad SERVES 4

Pasta shells - *100g (4oz)*
Cooked ham - *40g (1½ oz) diced*
Red pepper - *½, cored, de-seeded, diced*
Green pepper - *½, cored, de-seeded, diced*
Spring onions - *4, sliced*
Celery - *1 stick, diced*
Derby cheese - *50g (2oz) cubed*
Low calorie mayonnaise - *45ml (3 tbsp)*
Fresh single cream - *30ml (2 tbsp)*
Black pepper - *freshly ground*

METHOD

1 Cook pasta as directed on the packet.

2 Combine the ham, red and green pepper, spring onions, celery and cheese.

3 Blend mayonnaise and cream and season with black pepper. Coat the salad with the dressing and serve chilled.

475 Calories per portion

Sardine Tart   SERVES 4

Shortcrust pastry - *175g (6oz)*
Sardines in oil - *120g (4¼ oz) can*
Onion - *1 small, finely sliced*
Lemon - *½, juice only*
Natural yogurt - *75g (2½ oz) low fat*
Fresh single cream - *75ml (2½ fl oz)*
Cottage cheese - *50g (2oz)*
Eggs - *2 (size 3), beaten*
Salt *and freshly ground* **black pepper**
Parsley - *chopped for garnish*

METHOD

1 Roll out pastry and use to line a 18cm (7 inch)
flan ring.

2 Drain oil from the sardines and use to fry the
onion until soft. Arrange in the flan ring and
sprinkle with half the lemon juice.

3 Blend yogurt, cream, cottage cheese and eggs together,
season with black pepper and pour into flan case. Arrange sardines
on top, so they form the spokes of a wheel and sprinkle
with the remaining lemon juice. Bake at 200°C (400°F), mark 7 for
15 minutes then reduce the temperature to 180°C (350°F), mark 4
for a further 15-20 minutes or until golden. Serve garnished with parsley.

---

350 Calories per portion

Sardine Supper   SERVES 4

Sardines in oil - *2 x 120g (4¼ oz) cans, drained*
Tomatoes - *2, skinned and sliced*
Spring onions - *6, chopped*
Lemon juice - *30ml (2 tbsp)*
Black pepper - *freshly ground*
Butter - *15g (½ oz)*
Plain flour - *25g (1oz)*
Fresh milk - *300ml (½ pint)*
English Cheddar cheese - *100g (4oz) grated*
Wholemeal breadcrumbs - *25g (1oz)*
Spring onions - *2, chopped to garnish*

METHOD

1 Flake sardines into a shallow ovenproof dish. Cover
with tomatoes and spring onions, sprinkle with lemon
juice and season lightly.

2 Place butter, flour and milk in a saucepan, heat stirring
continuously until the sauce thickens and boils. Cook for
one minute. Remove from the heat, stir in half the cheese,
season lightly and pour over the sardines.

3 Mix remaining cheese with the breadcrumbs, sprinkle
over the sauce and bake at 200°C (400°F), mark 7 for
15-20 minutes or until golden. Serve garnished with
chopped spring onions:

515 Calories per portion

Mackerel Provençal SERVES 4

Fresh mackerel - *4 x 175g (6oz) whole*
Butter - *15g (½ oz) plus a little to brush the fish*
Onion - *1 small, chopped*
Plain flour - *25g (1oz)*
Fresh milk - *150ml (¼ pint)*
Chopped tomatoes - *400g (14oz) can*
Garlic clove - *1, crushed*
Bouquet garni
Salt *and freshly ground* **black pepper**
Watercress - *to garnish*

METHOD

1 Wash, gut and clean the mackerel. Brush
with a little melted butter and cook under a
pre-heated grill for about 5-8 minutes on each
side. Keep hot.

2 Gently fry the onion in the butter until soft.
Stir in the flour. Blend in the milk, tomatoes, garlic
and bouquet garni, season lightly then bring to the boil.
Simmer gently for 15 minutes. Remove bouquet garni and pour
into a sauce boat.

3 Serve mackerel garnished with watercress, accompanied by the sauce.

475 Calories per portion

Baked Mackerel with Yogurt SERVES 4

Fresh mackerel - *4 x 175g (6oz) whole*
Natural yogurt - *150g (5oz) low fat*
Fresh double cream - *60ml (4 tbsp)*
Salt *and freshly ground* **black pepper**
Lemon and watercress - *to garnish*

METHOD

1 Wash, gut and clean the mackerel, dry them
well and place in an ovenproof dish.

2 Blend the yogurt and cream, season lightly and
pour over the fish. Bake at 190°C (375°F), mark 5
for 20-25 minutes or until the fish is tender.
Serve garnished with lemon and watercress.

450 Calories per portion Ⓕ

Tuna & Watercress Croquettes SERVES 4

Natural yogurt - *150g (5oz)*
Fresh single cream - *30ml (2 tbsp)*
Lemon juice - *15ml (3 tsp)*
Caster sugar - *2.5ml (½ tsp)*
Watercress - *45ml (3 tbsp), finely chopped*
Salt *and freshly ground* **black pepper**
Fresh milk - *300ml (½ pint)*
Instant mashed potato - *131g (4¾ oz) packet*
Canned tuna - *198g (7oz) can, drained and flaked*
Eggs - *2 (size 3) beaten*

Breadcrumbs - *75g (3oz)*
Oil - *for shallow drying*
Lemon wedges - *for garnish*

METHOD

1 Blend yogurt, cream, lemon juice, sugar and 30ml (2 tbsp) chopped watercress in a basin. Season lightly and chill.

2 Heat the milk to boiling point, stir in the instant mashed potato and mix well. Stir in the remaining watercress, tuna and one beaten egg. Chill for 30 minutes.

3 On a floured surface, shape the tuna mixture into a roll and cut into 8 slices. Shape each into a croquette, dip into the remaining egg then coat in breadcrumbs.

4 Heat some oil in a frying pan, add the croquettes and fry for 3-4 minutes on each side or until cooked through. Serve with lemon wedges and the watercress sauce.

---

280 Calories per slice

Sandwich Gateau MAKES 14 SLICES

Cornflour - *25g (1oz)*
Fresh milk - *300ml (½ pint)*
Salt *and freshly ground* **black pepper**
Butter - *100g (4oz) softened*
Canned salmon - *90g (3½ oz) can, drained and flaked*
Cucumber - *2.5cm (1 inch) piece, chopped*
Red Leicester - *75g (3oz) finely grated*
Chives - *15ml (1 tbsp) chopped*
Marmite - *5ml (1 tsp)*
Large wholemeal loaf - *1, unsliced, crust removed*

Curd cheese - *350g (12oz) softened*
Stuffed olives and hazelnuts - *for garnish*

METHOD

1 Blend cornflour and milk, heat to boiling point and simmer for 2 minutes. Season lightly, cover and cool. Beat in the softened butter using an electric beater.

2 To one third of the sauce add salmon and cucumber, to another cheese and chives, add Marmite to the third.

3 Slice the loaf lengthwise into 7 slices. Spread the mixtures over two slices of bread each. Layer up the slices, then top with the last slice. Cover with foil and chill.

4 Mix the curd cheese with enough milk to give a spreadable consistency. Use two thirds to cover the top and sides of the 'gateau'. Fill a piping bag with the remainder and decorate. Garnish with sliced olives and nuts.

—— *Fish* ——

470 Calories per portion

Fish Risotto & Parsley Sauce SERVES 4

Cod - *100g (4oz)*
Fresh milk - *300ml (½ pint)*
Onion - *175g (6oz)*
Butter - *40g (1½ oz)*
Long grain rice - *175g (6oz)*
Canned tuna - *200g (7oz can, drained and flaked)*
Tomatoes - *4, skinned and chopped*
Cucumber - *¼, chopped*
Salt *and freshly ground* **black pepper**
Plain flour - *25g (1oz)*
Parsley - *15ml (1 tbsp) chopped*

METHOD

1 Poach the cod in the milk. Drain and reserve the liquor.

2 Gently fry the onion in 25g (1oz) butter until soft. Add the rice, fry a further 5 minutes then add 568ml (1 pint) water. Simmer for 15-20 minutes or until all the water has been absorbed and the rice is tender. Add flaked cod, tuna, tomatoes and cucumber and season lightly.

3 Place the fish liquor, flour and remaining butter in a saucepan, heat stirring continuously until the sauce thickens and boils. Cook for one minute, then add parsley and serve with the risotto.

---

230 Calories per portion

Stilton Salad Ring SERVES 6

Stilton cheese - *100g (4oz), crumbled*
Mayonnaise - *75ml (5 tbsp)*
Lemon juice - *10ml (2 tsp)*
Gelatine - *11g sachet*
Canned salmon - *215g (7½ oz) can, drained and flaked*
Cucumber - *50g (2oz) chopped*
Celery - *50g (2oz) chopped*
Onion - *1 small, finely chopped*
Salt *and freshly ground*
Black pepper
Watercress - *1 small bunch*

METHOD

1 Cream Stilton with 15ml (1 tbsp) mayonnaise, the lemon juice and 15ml (1 tbsp) water.

2 Sprinkle gelatine over 60ml (4 tbsp) hot water in a basin. Place basin over a pan of simmering water and stir until dissolved.

3 Stir 10ml (2 tsp) dissolved gelatine into the Stilton mixture and pour into a wetted 568ml (1 pint) ring mould. Leave for about 15 minutes to set.

4 Combine salmon, cucumber, celery and onion with the remaining mayonnaise, season lightly and stir in the remaining gelatine. Spoon carefully into the ring mould. Chill well.

5 Remove the ring by dipping quickly in hot water and invert onto a serving plate. Fill centre with watercress.

25

190 Calories per portion

Fisherman's Platter SERVES 4

Cottage cheese - *225g (8oz)*
Fresh single cream - *75ml (5 tbsp)*
Prawns - *225g (8oz) fresh or frozen (thawed)*
Celery - *4 sticks, chopped*
Green pepper - *½ small, chopped*
Black pepper - *freshly ground*
Lettuce - *for serving*
Canned pineapple rings - *225g (8oz) can, drained*
Paprika and parsley - *for garnish*

METHOD

1 Mix cottage cheese, cream, prawns, celery and green pepper. Season well with black pepper and chill.

2 Arrange lettuce on 4 serving plates and divide the prawn mixture between them. Decorate with halved pineapple rings. Sprinkle with paprika and parsley before serving.

490 Calories per portion Ⓕ

Cheddar Haddock Pie SERVES 6

Plain flour - *250g (9oz)*
Butter - *150g (5oz) in small cubes*
Lancashire cheese - *75g (3oz) finely grated*
Egg - *1 (size 3) beaten*
Smoked haddock - *350g (12oz)*
Fresh milk - *300ml (½ pint)*
Parsley - *45ml (3 tbsp) chopped*
Fresh milk - *to glaze the pie*

METHOD

1 Place 225g (8oz) flour in a basin and rub in 100g (4oz) butter until the mixture resembles fine breadcrumbs. Stir in the cheese. Blend in the egg, adding a little milk if necessary, to form a dough. Knead lightly and divide in two. Use half the pastry to line a 23cm (9 inch) plate.

2 Place fish and milk in saucepan, simmer for 15 minutes or until the fish flakes easily. Drain, reserving the liquor.

3 Place liquor, remaining flour and butter in a saucepan, heat stirring continuously until the sauce thickens and boils. Cook for one minute then add the fish and parsley. Pour into the pastry case.

4 Use remaining pastry to cover the pie and bake at 190°C (375°F), mark 5 for 25-30 minutes until golden.

310 Calories per portion

Tange Marine SERVES 4

Cod fillets - *450g (1lb) skinned*
Wholemeal breadcrumbs - *50g (2oz)*
Dried tarragon - *5ml (1 tsp)*
Oranges - *2, juice and rind*
Egg - *1 (size 3) beaten*
Butter - *15g (½ oz)*

Plain flour - *25g (1oz)*
Fresh milk - *300ml (½ pint)*
Salt *and freshly ground* **black pepper**
Fresh single cream - *150ml (5 fl oz)*
Orange and parsley - *for garnish*

METHOD

1 Arrange half the fish in an ovenproof dish.

2 Mix the breadcrumbs, tarragon, orange rind and just enough egg to bind, sprinkle mixture over the fish. Arrange the remaining fish on top.

3 Pour over the orange juice and add diced butter. Cover and bake at 190°C (375°F), mark 5 for 25 minutes or until the fish is tender. Drain the juices into a saucepan, cover the fish and keep it warm.

4 Blend the flour in a cup with a little milk until smooth. Stir into the juices in the pan, add the remaining milk then heat stirring continuously until the sauce thickens and boils. Cook for one minute. Season lightly. Stir in cream with any remaining egg. Reheat without boiling.

5 Pour a little sauce over the fish, garnish with sliced orange and parsley. Serve remaining sauce separately.

490 Calories per portion

A Fishy Tale SERVES 4

English Cheddar cheese - *175g (6oz) finely grated*
Mashed potato - *350g (12oz)*
Eggs - *4 (size 3) beaten*
Fresh milk - *150ml (¼ pint)*
Fresh white breadcrumbs - *50g (2oz)*
Butter - *15g (½ oz)*
Smoked haddock - *350g (12oz) poached and flaked*
Salt *and freshly ground* **black pepper**
Tomato and parsley - *for garnish*

METHOD

1 Mash half the cheese into the potato until smooth. Spoon into a piping bag fitted with a vegetable star nozzle. Pipe the outline of a fish shape onto a large oval ovenproof plate then continue piping over the outline to form a deep rim.

2 Brush potato with a little egg and bake at 200°C (400°F), mark 6 until golden.

3 Add the milk, breadcrumbs and the remaining cheese to the beaten eggs. Season lightly. Melt the butter in a saucepan, add the egg mixture and cook, stirring until scrambled. Stir in the fish and heat gently.

4 Pile the mixture into the potato border and serve garnished with sliced tomato and parsley.

480 Calories per portion

Cheesy Fish Bake SERVES 4

Cod fillets - *375g (12oz) skinned*
Fresh milk - *300ml (½ pint)*
Bay leaf - *1*
Salt *and freshly ground* **black pepper**
Plain flour - *25g (1oz)*
Butter - *25g (1oz)*
English Cheddar cheese - *150g (5oz) finely grated*
New potatoes - *700g (1½ lb) cooked and sliced*
Anchovy fillets - *50g (2oz) can, drained*

METHOD

1 Place fish and milk in a saucepan, add bay leaf
and season lightly. Cover and poach gently for
10-15 minutes or until the fish flakes. Drain,
reserving the juices.

2 Place juices, flour and butter in a saucepan, heat
stirring continuously until sauce thickens and boils.
Cook for one minute. Remove from the heat, stir in
half the grated cheese and the flaked fish.

3 Arrange half the potatoes in the base of a greased
ovenproof dish, cover with the fish sauce, then top with the
remaining potatoes and grated cheese. Make a lattice on top with
anchovies. Bake at 200°C (400°F), mark 6 for 15-20 minutes or until golden.

---

400 Calories per portion

Special Fish Bake SERVES 4

Potatoes - *700g (1½ lb) peeled and cooked*
Fresh milk - *for mashed potato*
Butter - *15g (½ oz)*
Plain flour - *25g (1oz)*
Fresh milk - *300ml (½ pint)*
Salt *and freshly ground* **black pepper**
Salad cream - *30ml (2 tbsp)*
Gherkins - *2 large, sliced*
Lemon juice - *5ml (1 tsp)*
Coley or other white fish - *350g (12oz)*
Tomatoes - *2, large sliced*
English Cheddar cheese - *50g (2oz) finely grated*
Parsley - *for garnish*

METHOD

1 Mash potatoes with a little milk to give a piping consistency.
Place in a piping bag fitted with a vegetable star nozzle.

2 Place butter, flour and milk in a saucepan, heat stirring
continuously until the sauce thickens and boils. Cook for
one minute. Season lightly then stir in the salad cream,
gherkins and lemon juice.

3 Arrange fish in the base of a greased overproof dish. Cover with
sauce and the sliced tomatoes. Pipe potato over the top and sprinkle with
cheese. Bake at 190°C (375°F), mark 5 for 30 minutes. Serve garnished with parsley.

535 Calories per portion

Golden Cod SERVES 4

Cod fillet - *350g (12oz)*
Fresh milk - *75ml (5 tbsp)*
CHEESE SAUCE
Butter - *25g (1oz)*
Plain flour - *40g (1½ oz)*
Fresh milk - *300ml (½ pint)*
Salt *and freshly ground* **black pepper**
English Cheddar cheese - *75g (3oz) finely grated*

Button mushrooms - *75g (3oz) sliced*
Butter - *20g (¾ oz)*
Brown rice - *225g (8oz)*

4 Cook rice according to the instructions on the packet. Arrange around the edge of a warm serving dish, pile fish mixture into the centre and serve garnished with the mushrooms.

METHOD

1 Poach the cod in 75ml (5 tbsp) milk over a gentle heat for about 10 minutes or until tender. Drain fish, reserving the juices.

2 Place fish juices, butter, flour and milk in a saucepan and heat, stirring continuously until the sauce thickens and boils. Season lightly and cook for one minute. Remove the pan from the heat and stir in the cheese. Fold in the flaked fish. Keep warm.

3 Gently fry the mushrooms in the 20g (¾ oz) butter.

280 Calories per portion **Ⓕ**

Curried Cod Cutlets SERVES 4

Onion - *1 small, chopped*
Mushrooms - *50g (2oz) sliced*
Green pepper - *½, finely chopped*
Curry powder - *10ml (2 tsp)*
Butter - *40g (1½ oz)*
Canned tomatoes - *400g (14oz) can*
Sugar - *5ml (1 tsp)*
Salt *and freshly ground* **black pepper**
Cornflour - *15ml (1 tbsp)*
Fresh milk - *150ml (¼ pint)*
Cod cutlets - *4 x 100g (4oz) each*

Lemon juice - *60ml (4 tbsp)*
Parsley - *for garnish*

METHOD

1 Fry onion, mushrooms, pepper and curry powder in 25g (1oz) butter until soft. Add tomatoes and sugar, season lightly.

2 Blend the cornflour with 30ml (2 tbsp) milk and pour into a saucepan with remaining milk. Stir in the tomato mixture, bring to the boil, simmer for 10 minutes.

3 Dot cutlets with remaining butter, sprinkle with lemon juice and grill on both sides until tender.

4 Pour sauce onto a warmed serving dish, arrange fish on top and garnish with parsley.

180 Calories per portion

Fish Mediterranean SERVES 4

Onion - *1 small, finely chopped*
Butter - *15g (½ oz)*
Mushrooms - *75g (3oz) sliced*
Tomatoes - *2 small, skinned and chopped*
Fresh white breadcrumbs - *25g (1oz)*
Parsley - *15ml (1 tbsp) chopped*
Salt *and freshly ground* **black pepper**

Cod steaks - *4 x 100g (4oz) each*
Lemon - *½, juice and rind*
Dried thyme - *large pinch*
Black peppercorns - *6*
Cornflour - *15g (½ oz)*
Natural yogurt - *150g (5oz) low fat*
Tomato and watercress - *for garnish*

METHOD

1 Gently fry the onion in the butter for 1 minute. Add the mushrooms, tomatoes, breadcrumbs and parsley and season lightly.

2 Make a slit along each cod steak and fill with stuffing. Arrange in the base of a greased ovenproof dish, sprinkle with lemon juice and rind, 60ml (4 tbsp) water, thyme and peppercorns. Cover and cook at 170°C (325°F), mark 3 for 30 minutes. Drain fish, reserve the juices. Cover the fish and keep warm.

3 Pour the juices into a saucepan. Blend the cornflour with 30ml (2 tbsp) water and add to the juices. Heat, stirring continuously until the sauce thickens and boils. Season lightly and cook for one minute. Stir in the yogurt, reheat gently and pour over the fish. Serve garnished with tomato and watercress.

445 Calories per portion (F)

Cheese & Haddock Hotpot SERVES 4

Haddock fillets - *450g (1lb)*
Mushrooms - *100g (4oz) sliced*
Butter - *40g (1½ oz)*
Plain flour - *40g (1½ oz)*
Fresh milk - *300ml (½ pint)*
Salt *and freshly ground* **black pepper**
English Cheddar cheese - *100g (4oz)*
Onion - *½ small, chopped*
Potatoes - *2 medium, thinly sliced*
Parsley - *chopped for garnish*

METHOD

1 Arrange haddock in the base of a greased ovenproof dish and scatter mushrooms over the top.

2 Place butter, flour and milk in a saucepan, heat stirring continuously until the sauce thickens and boils. Season lightly and cook for one minute. Remove from the heat and stir in 75g (3oz) cheese and the onion. Pour sauce over the fish.

3 Arrange sliced potato over the sauce, season lightly, sprinkle with the remaining cheese and bake at 200°C (400°F), mark 6 for 40-50 minutes. Serve garnished with parsley.

390 Calories per portion

Plaice with Stilton SERVES 4

Stilton cheese - *75g (3oz) crumbled*
Fresh breadcrumbs - *50g (2oz)*
Onion - *1 small, chopped*
Salt *and freshly ground* **black pepper**
Plaice fillets - *4 x 150g (6oz) each*
Fresh milk - *300ml (½ pint)*
Butter - *15g (½ oz)*
Plain flour - *15g (½ oz)*
Fresh single cream - *30ml (2 tbsp)*
Lemon juice - *10ml (2 tsp)*

METHOD

1 Mix the Stilton, breadcrumbs and onion. Season lightly and divide into 4 balls.

2 Wrap a plaice fillet around each ball of stuffing and place in the base of a greased ovenproof dish. Pour milk over the fish, cover and bake at 190°C (375°F), mark 5 for 20 minutes. Remove fish and reserve juices. Cover fish and keep warm.

3 Place fish juices, butter and flour in a saucepan, heat stirring continuously until sauce thickens and boils. Cook for one minute. Stir in the fresh cream and lemon juice. Pour sauce over the fish and serve immediately.

---

485 Calories per portion (F)

Family Fish Pie SERVES 4

Butter - *25g (1oz)*
Plain flour - *50g (2oz)*
Fresh milk - *568ml (1 pint)*
Smoked haddock - *350g (12oz) skinned and cubed*
Frozen peas - *100g (4oz)*
Canned sweetcorn - *198g (7oz) can, drained*
Egg - *1 (size 3), hardboiled and chopped*
Chopped parsley - *15ml (1 tbsp)*
Potatoes - *450g (1lb) peeled and cooked*
Swede - *225g (8oz) peeled and cooked*
Butter - *7g (¼ oz)*

METHOD

1 Place the butter, flour and milk in a saucepan. Heat, stirring continuously, until the sauce thickens, boils and is smooth. Add the fish, peas, sweetcorn, egg and parsley and cook for 5 minutes. Transfer to an ovenproof dish.

2 Mash potatoes and swede with a little milk. Heat through and spoon over the fish. Swirl the surface with a fork, dot with butter and place under a hot grill until golden.

655 Calories per portion Ⓕ

Chicken Maryland Pie SERVES 4

Onion - *1 small, chopped*
Red pepper - *1, chopped*
Butter - *50g (2oz)*
Plain flour - *50g (2oz)*
Fresh milk - *300ml (½ pint)*
Salt *and freshly ground* **black pepper**
Canned sweetcorn - *198g (7oz) drained*
Cooked chicken - *225g (8oz) cubed*
Bananas - *3 medium, sliced*
Frozen puff pastry - *215g (7½ oz) packet, thawed*
Egg - *1, for brushing pastry*

METHOD

1 Gently fry onion and pepper in the butter until soft.
Add flour and stir in the milk, heat stirring continuously
until sauce thickens, boils and is smooth. Cook for
one minute, season then add sweetcorn and chicken.
Place in the base of an ovenproof dish, cover with
a layer of banana.

2 Roll out pastry and use to cover the mixture. Brush
with beaten egg. Bake at 220°C (425°F), mark 7 for
30 minutes until golden.

---

695 Calories per portion

Chicken Parisienne SERVES 4

Frozen puff pastry - *400g (14oz) packet, thawed*
Butter - *50g (2oz)*
Onion - *1 small, sliced*
Green pepper - *1 cored and de-seeded*
Courgettes - *225g (8oz) sliced*
Aubergine - *1, sliced*

Dried mixed herbs - *2.5ml (½ tsp)*
Tomato purée - *30ml (2 tbsp)*
Salt *and freshly ground* **pepper**
Plain flour - *25g (1 oz)*
Fresh milk - *300ml (½ pint)*
Cooked chicken - *175g (6oz) cubed*
Tomato - *1 sliced, to garnish*

METHOD

1 Roll out pastry to 20.5 x 27.5cm (8 x 11 inches). Fold in half lengthwise so that ends meet. Cut a border
2.5cm (1 inch) inside the three open edges, cutting through both folds. Remove edge and open out to form
a frame. Roll out remaining rectangle so removed frame fits on top. Place rectangle on wetted baking sheet,
brush edges with water and place the frame on top.
Make a criss-cross pattern on the frame with a knife.

2 Bake at 220°C (425°F), mark 7 for 15-20 minutes
until well risen. Press down the inner layer. Return
to the oven for a few minutes to dry out.

3 Melt 25g (1oz) butter in a large saucepan, add the
onion, pepper, courgettes, aubergine, herbs and
tomato purée. Season lightly. Fry gently for 5 minutes
then cover and simmer for 15 minutes until tender.

4 Put remaining butter, flour and milk into a large saucepan,
heat stirring continuously until the sauce thickens, boils and is
smooth. Cook for one minute then stir in the chicken and vegetables.
Re-heat thoroughly. Pour into the pastry case and garnish with tomato.

430 Calories per portion

Chicken Cheddar Choux SERVES 6

CHOUX
Butter - *50g (2oz)*
Fresh milk - *150ml (¼ pint)*
Plain flour - *65g (2½ oz) sieved*
Eggs - *2 (size 3), beaten*
English Cheddar - *100g (4oz) finely grated*

FILLING
Onion - *1 small, chopped*
Butter - *25g (1 oz)*
Plain flour - *25g (1oz)*
Fresh milk - *300ml (½ pint)*
English Cheddar - *50g (2oz) grated*
Black pepper - *freshly ground*
Cooked chicken - *225g (8oz) cubed*

METHOD

1 To make choux: place butter and milk in a saucepan and bring to the boil. Remove from the heat and tip in flour all at once. Beat until smooth and forms a ball. Beat in eggs a little at a time, beating well after each addition. Beat in the cheese.

2 Pipe choux around the edge of a greased flan dish and bake at 200°C (400°F), mark 6 for 30-35 minutes until golden.

3 Sauce: sauté onion in the butter, add flour and milk and heat, stirring until boiling. Remove from the heat, add the cheese, pepper and chicken. Heat thoroughly and fill centre of the choux ring. Serve immediately.

---

535 Calories per portion

Christmas Star SERVES 4

Potatoes - *1kg (2.2lb) cooked and mashed*
Egg - *1 beaten, for brushing potatoes*
Butter - *25g (1oz)*
Onion - *1 small, finely chopped*
Button mushrooms - *100g (4oz) halved*
Plain flour - *40g (1½ oz)*
Fresh milk - *450ml (¾ pint)*
Red pepper - *1, cored, de-seeded, diced*
Cooked chicken or turkey - *225g (8oz) chopped*
Sherry - *45ml (3 tbsp)*
Salt *and freshly ground* **black pepper**
Parsley - *sprigs for garnish*

METHOD

1 Pipe or mould potato into a star on a greased ovenproof plate and spread remaining potato on the base of the plate. Place under a hot grill and once potato is firm, brush lightly with egg then return to the grill until golden.

2 Meanwhile, melt butter in a saucepan and gently fry onion and mushrooms until tender. Add flour and milk and heat stirring continuously until sauce thickens and boils. Add pepper, meat and sherry. Season and simmer gently for 10 minutes. Pile mixture in the centre of the star and serve garnished with parsley

410 Calories per portion

Parsley and Thyme Flan   SERVES 4

Parsley and thyme stuffing mix - *1 packet*
Boiling water - *200ml (7 fl oz)*
Egg - *1 (size 3) beaten*
Butter - *75g (3 oz) melted*
Small button mushrooms - *225g (8oz)*
Plain flour - *25g (1oz)*
Fresh milk - *300ml (½ pint)*
Salt *and freshly ground* **black pepper**
Cooked chicken - *175g (6oz) diced*
Stuffed olives - *sliced for garnish*

METHOD

1 Place stuffing mix in a basin, stir in the boiling water, egg and 50g (2oz) melted butter. Leave to stand for 5 minutes then press into a greased 20cm (8 inch) flan ring. Bake at 190°C (375°F), mark 5 for 20 minutes.

2 Place remaining butter in a saucepan and fry mushrooms until tender. Add flour and milk, heat stirring continuously until the sauce thickens, boils and is smooth. Cook for one minute, season lightly and add chicken. Heat thoroughly and pour into the flan case. Serve garnished with olives.

345 Calories per portion Ⓕ

Spicy Chicken Chantilly   SERVES 4

Onion - *1 small, chopped*
Red pepper - *1, cored de-seeded and chopped*
Butter - *25g (1oz)*
Chilli powder - *5ml (1 tsp)*
Fresh milk - *150ml (¼ pint)*
Tomato purée - *15ml (1 tbsp)*
Lemon juice - *15ml (1 tbsp)*
Sultanas - *25g (1oz)*
Chicken stock cube - *1, crumbled*
Black pepper - *freshly ground*
Natural yogurt - *150g (5oz) low fat*
Canned apricots - *411g (14½ oz) drained and puréed*
Cooked chicken - *275g (10oz) chopped*
Parsley - *chopped for garnish*

METHOD

1 Gently fry the onion and pepper in the butter until soft. Add chilli powder and cook for 1 minute. Add milk, tomato purée, lemon juice, sultanas and stock cube. Simmer for 10 minutes.

2 Blend yogurt and apricot purée. Stir into the sauce with the chicken. Reheat thoroughly and serve garnished with parsley.

270 Calories per portion

Honey Barbecued Chicken SERVES 4

Butter - *50g (2 oz)*
Onion - *100g (4oz) finely chopped*
Garlic clove - *1 finely chopped*
Canned tomatoes - *400g (14oz) can*
Worcestershire sauce - *30ml (2 tbsp)*
Honey - *15ml (1tbsp)*
Black pepper - *freshly ground*
Chicken drumsticks - *4 large or 8 small*
Grilled mushrooms,
Tomatoes and watercress - *for garnish*

METHOD

1 Combine butter, onions, garlic, tomatoes, Worcestershire sauce, honey and black pepper in a saucepan. Simmer gently for 30 minutes.

2 Place drumsticks in a grill pan, brush liberally with sauce and grill for about 10 minutes, frequently turning and brushing with extra sauce. Be sure the drumsticks are thoroughly cooked through. Serve garnished with mushrooms, tomatoes and watercress.

---

415 Calories per portion

Peppered Chicken SERVES 4

Chicken portions - *4 skinned and boned*
Butter - *25g (1oz)*
Chicken stock - *300ml (½ pint)*
Dried mixed herbs - *pinch*
Bay leaf - *1*
Fresh milk - *300ml (½ pint)*
Salt *and freshly ground* **black pepper**
Long grain rice - *100g (4oz)*
Green pepper - *1 small, chopped*
Red pepper - *1 small, chopped*
Onion - *1 small finely chopped*
Tomatoes - *2 skinned and chopped*

Button mushrooms - *50g (2oz) sliced*
Tomato purée - *15ml (1 tbsp)*
Watercress - *for garnish*

METHOD

1 Fry chicken pieces in the butter in a large saucepan until brown on all sides. Add stock, herbs, bay leaf and milk. Season lightly. Bring almost to the boil, simmer for 20 minutes.

2 Add rice, peppers, onion, tomatoes, mushrooms and tomato purée. Cook for 20 minutes or until chicken and rice are cooked and all liquid is absorbed. Serve immediately, garnished with watercress.

340 Calories per portion

Savoury Pancakes SERVES 4

Plain flour - *100g (4oz)*
Fresh milk - *300ml (½ pint)*
Eggs - *2 (size 3) beaten*
Onion - *1 small, finely chopped*
Celery - *3 sticks, finely chopped*
Butter - *15g (½ oz)*
Cooked chicken - *100g (4oz) chopped*
Prawns - *100g (4oz)*
Mushrooms - *100g (4oz)*
Black pepper - *freshly ground*

Cornflour - *10ml (2 tsp)*
Water - *150ml (¼ pint)*
Lemon juice - *10ml (2 tsp)*
Soy sauce - *10ml (2 tsp)*
Frozen peas - *75g (3oz) cooked*
Bean sprouts - *75g (3oz)*

METHOD

1 Sift flour into a basin, blend in a little of the milk, add the beaten eggs then whisk in the rest of the milk. Use to make 8 medium sized pancakes.

2 Fry onion and celery in the butter and cook for 2 minutes. Add the chicken, prawns, mushrooms and black pepper. Cook for 3 minutes.

3 Blend the cornflour, water, lemon juice and soy sauce, add to the saucepan and cook until boiling. Stir in the peas and beansprouts.

4 Place some mixture onto a quarter of each pancake. Fold in half then fold that half over again to form a pocket which encloses the filling. Serve immediately.

---

595 Calories per portion

Coronation Chicken SERVES 4

Butter mushrooms - *175g (6oz) thickly sliced*
Chicken stock - *200ml (7 fl oz)*
Shallots - *4, finely chopped*
Butter - *25g (1oz)*
Plain flour - *25g (1oz)*
Fresh double cream - *225ml (8 fl oz)*
Salt *and freshly ground* **black pepper**
Tomatoes - *450g (1lb) skinned and chopped*
Cooked chicken breasts - *4 without skin*
Red Leicester cheese - *50g (2oz)*

METHOD

1 Cook mushrooms in the stock, simmering until the stock is reduced to 45ml (3 tbsp). Remove the mushrooms. Add shallots to stock, cook until soft.

2 Place butter and flour in a saucepan and cook for 2 minutes. Gradually add the cream and cook, stirring continuously until the sauce thickens. Season lightly then add the shallots and tomatoes and cook for 5 minutes.

3 Arrange the chicken in an ovenproof dish and cover with mushrooms. Pour over the sauce, sprinkle with cheese and bake at 200°C (400°F), mark 6 for 20-30 minutes until golden.

560 Calories per portion

Candlelight Chicken SERVES 2

Chicken breasts - *2 with wing bone attached*
Sage and onion stuffing - *30ml (2 tbsp) ready made*
Onion - *1 small, chopped*
Butter - *15g (½ oz)*
Chicken stock - *150ml (¼ pint)*
Fresh milk - *150ml (¼ pint)*

Dry white wine - *150ml (¼ pint)*
Plain flour - *15g (½ oz)*
Fresh single cream - *150ml (5 fl oz)*
Asparagus spears - *225g (8oz) canned, drained*
Croûtes - *to garnish*

METHOD

1 Remove bones from the breasts with a sharp knife, leaving the wing bone in position. Flatten between damp sheets of greaseproof paper with a rolling pin.

2 Place 15ml (1 tbsp) stuffing in the centre of each breast then roll breast round to enclose stuffing. Secure with a cocktail stick.

3 Fry onion in the butter until transparent then add chicken breasts and cook, turning, until golden. Place chicken in an ovenproof dish.

4 Add stock, milk and wine to the onion, bring to the boil and simmer for 5-10 minutes. Pour over the chicken. Bake at 180°C (350°F), mark 4 for 45 minutes. Remove the cocktail sticks.

5 Blend the flour with a little cream then add remaining cream and 30ml (2 tbsp) of the cooking liquor. Add to the casserole with the asparagus and return to the oven for 10 minutes. Serve garnished with heart shaped croûtes.

390 Calories per portion 🅕

Chicken Casserole SERVES 4

Butter - *25g (1oz)*
Chicken joints - *4 without skin*
Baby onions - *8 small*
Red pepper - *1 de-seeded and chopped*
Condensed mushroom soup - *300g (10.6oz) can*
Fresh milk - *150ml (¼ pint)*
Bay leaf - *1*
Fresh single cream - *150ml (5 fl oz)*
Black pepper - *freshly ground*
Parsley - *chopped to garnish*

METHOD

1 Melt the butter in a large saucepan and fry chicken joints until golden on all sides. Add onions and red pepper and cook for 15 minutes.

2 Stir in the soup, milk and bay leaf. Cover, bring to the boil and simmer for 45 minutes or until chicken is thoroughly cooked. Stir in the cream and a little black pepper. Remove bay leaf and serve garnished with parsley.

700 Calories in the stuffing recipe

Roast Chicken with Cheese and Peanut Stuffing

SERVES 4-6

Roasting chicken - *approx 1.6kg (3½ lb)*
Fresh breadcrumbs - *50g(2oz)*
English Cheddar cheese - *100g (4oz) grated*
Celery - *1 stick, chopped*
Salted peanuts - *50g (2oz) chopped*
Onion - *1 small, chopped*
Black pepper - *freshly ground*
Egg - *1 (size 3) beaten*
Lemon juice - *10ml (2 tsp)*

METHOD

1 Mix the breadcrumbs, grated cheese, celery, peanuts and onion in a basin. Season lightly with black pepper and bind with beaten egg and lemon juice. Use to stuff the chicken, making stuffing balls with any excess mixture.

2 Place chicken in a roasting tin. Bake at 190°C (375°F) mark 5 for 1½ hours-2 hours, based on the stuffed weight of the bird. Add stuffing balls to the tin, 20 minutes before the end of the cooking time.

505 Calories per portion ⑥

Poussin à la Crème   SERVES 4

Lemon - *1, juice and rind*
Olive oil - *30ml (2 tbsp)*
Garlic clove - *1, crushed*
Black pepper - *freshly ground*
Dried tarragon - *5ml (1 tsp)*
Dry white wine - *150ml (¼ pint)*
Chicken stock cube - *1, crumbled*
Plain flour - *30ml (2 tbsp)*
Poussin - *4 x 450g each*
Fresh double cream - *150ml (5 fl oz)*
Watercress and lemon slices - *to garnish*
Roasting bags - *2*

METHOD

1 Mix the lemon juice, rind, oil, garlic, a little black pepper, tarragon, wine and crumbled stock cube.

2 Divide the flour between the 2 roasting bags and shake to coat the sides. Put 2 poussin and half the wine mixture in each bag. Tie the end of each bag and pierce each bag twice. Bake as directed by the roasting bag instructions for about 40 minutes or until tender.

3 Snip the corner off each bag and drain liquor into a saucepan. Boil uncovered for 5 minutes. Remove from the heat and stir in the cream. Reheat without boiling. Arrange poussin on a serving plate, pour sauce over and garnish with watercress and lemon.

465 Calories per portion Ⓕ

Curried Turkey Pie   SERVES 4

Onion - *1 large, sliced*
Carrots - *2 medium, sliced*
Button mushrooms - *50g (2oz) sliced*
Butter - *75g (3oz)*
Sherry - *15ml (1 tbsp)*
Curry powder - *15ml (1 tbsp)*
Plain flour - *150g (5oz)*
Chicken stock - *150ml (¼ pint)*
Fresh milk - *150ml (¼ pint)*
Salt *and freshly ground* **black pepper**
Mango chutney - *10ml (2 tsp)*
Cooked turkey - *275g (10oz)*
Egg - *1 (size 3) beaten with a little milk*

Add sufficient water to mix into a dough. Knead lightly and roll out so that it will cover the pie plate.

3 Cover the turkey mixture with the pastry, brush with beaten egg and bake at 220°C (425°F), mark 7 for 25 minutes or until golden.

METHOD

1 Fry onion, carrots and mushrooms in 25g (1oz) butter until soft. Stir in the sherry, curry powder and 25g (1oz) flour and cook for 2 minutes. Gradually stir in the stock and milk and heat, stirring continuously until the mixture boils. Season lightly, add the mango chutney and turkey. Spoon into a 20.5cm (8 inch) deep pie plate.

2 Place the remaining flour in a basin, add a pinch of salt and remaining butter in pieces. Rub butter into the flour until the mixture resembles fine breadcrumbs.

---

355 Calories per portion

Turkey & Vegetable Roulade   SERVES 6

Fresh milk - *300ml (½ pint)*
Butter - *50g (2oz)*
Plain flour - *50g (2oz)*
Red Leicester cheese - *175g (6oz) finely grated*
Eggs - *3 (size 3) separated*
Dried mixed herbs - *2.5ml (½ tsp) heaped*
Salt *and freshly ground* **black pepper**
Cooked mixed vegetables -
    350g (12oz) carrots, potatoes, sprouts, etc
Lemon - *½, grated rind and juice*
Cooked turkey - *175g (6oz) chopped*
Cooked ham - *50g (2oz) chopped*
Mushrooms - *100g (4oz) sliced*
Parsley - *15ml (1 tbsp) chopped*
Tomatoes and spring onions - *for garnish*

METHOD

1 Grease and line a 23 x 33cm (9½ x 12½ inch) swiss roll tin.

2 Place milk, butter and flour in a large saucepan, heat stirring continuously until the sauce thickens and boils. Remove from the heat, stir in cheese and remove half the sauce from the pan.

3 Add egg yolks and herbs to sauce in the pan and season lightly. Purée the cooked vegetables in a processor or blender until smooth, add to the sauce. Whisk the egg whites until stiff, fold into the mixture and turn into swiss roll tin. Smooth surface and bake at 190°C (375°F), mark 5 for 30 minutes.

4 Place the remaining sauce in a large saucepan, stir in the lemon rind and juice, turkey, ham, mushrooms and parsley. Cover and simmer gently for 15 minutes. Season lightly.

5 Turn the roulade onto a piece of parchment paper and remove the lining paper. Quickly spread with the filling and roll up using the paper to help. Transfer to a serving plate and garnish with tomato and spring onions.

305 Calories per portion

Turkey à la King   SERVES 4

Green pepper - *150g (5oz) cored and chopped*
Butter - *40g (1½ oz)*
Button mushrooms - *100g (4oz) sliced*
Plain flour - *25g (1oz)*
Turkey or chicken stock - *150ml (¼ pint)*
Fresh milk - *200ml (⅓ pint)*

Cooked turkey - *225g (8oz) bite-sized pieces*
Salt *and freshly ground* **black pepper**
Fresh single cream - *75ml (2½ fl oz)*
Eggs - *2 (size 3), yolks only*
Dry sherry or lemon juice - *15ml (1 tbsp)*

METHOD

1 Gently fry the pepper in the butter for 5 minutes in a large saucepan. Add the mushrooms and fry a further 5 minutes. Remove from the pan.

2 Stir the flour into the butter remaining in the pan. Gradually add the stock and 150ml (¼ pint) milk. Heat, stirring continuously, until the sauce thickens and boils. Cook for one minute.

3 Add the pepper, mushrooms and turkey to the sauce. Lower the heat, cover the pan and simmer for 10 minutes.

4 Blend the remaining milk with the cream, egg yolks and sherry. Add to the pan and reheat without boiling. Serve immediately.

---

220 Calories per portion

Chilled Curried Chicken   SERVES 4

Butter - *15g (½ oz)*
Onion - *100g (4oz) chopped*
Curry powder - *5-10ml (1-2 tsp)*
Tomato purée - *10ml (2 tsp)*
Red wine - *100ml (4 fl oz)*
Bay leaf - *1*
Lemon juice - *30ml (2 tbsp)*
Dried apricots - *3, chopped*

Low calorie mayonnaise - *45ml (3 tbsp)*
Low fat fromage frais - *175g (6oz)*
Red pepper - *½, chopped*
Cooked chicken - *225g (8oz) diced*
Green grapes - *75g (3oz) de-seeded and halved*
Black pepper - *freshly ground*
Cucumber slices - *to garnish*

METHOD

1 Sauté the onion in the butter until soft. Stir in the curry powder, tomato purée, wine, bay leaf, lemon juice and apricots. Simmer, uncovered, for 8 minutes. Remove bay leaf. Purée in a food processor or blender.

2 Beat the purée into the mayonnaise and fromage frais. Fold in the red pepper, chicken, grapes and plenty of black pepper. Add more lemon juice if necessary, to give a coating consistency. Serve chilled, garnished with cucumber.

570 Calories per portion

Stilton Stuffed Chicken SERVES 4

Chicken breasts - *4 x 175g (6oz) with wing bone attached*
Blue Stilton - *100g (4oz)*
Butter - *25g (1oz)*
Garlic clove - *1, chopped*
Lemon juice - *15ml (1 tbsp)*

Plain flour - *25g (1oz)*
Egg - *1 (size 3) beaten*
Dried breadcrumbs - *for coating*
Fresh sage leaves - *for garnish*

METHOD

1 Skin the chicken breasts. Remove the bones with a sharp knife, leaving the wing bone in position. Flatten between damp sheets of greaseproof paper with a rolling pin.

2 Blend the Stilton, butter, garlic and lemon juice. Divide between the chicken breasts and roll the breasts round to enclose the stuffing. Secure with a cocktail stick.

3 Toss the breasts in flour, dip in the egg and coat in breadcrumbs. Chill for 2 hours to allow the coating to dry.

4 Heat the oil in a deep fat fryer to 160°C (325°F). Cook two breasts at a time for 15 minutes until brown and firm when pressed with a fork. Do not prick with a fork or the filling will escape! Drain and remove cocktail sticks before serving.

275 Calories per portion

Chicken Cacciatore SERVES 4

Chicken portions - *4 x 225g (8oz)*
Plain flour - *30ml (2 tbsp)*
Salt *and freshly ground* **black pepper**
Butter - *25g (1oz)*
Onion - *1 large, chopped*
Garlic clove - *1, chopped*
Tomatoes - *450g (1lb) skinned and chopped*
Sugar - *5ml (1 tsp)*
Chicken stock - *150ml (¼ pint)*
Button mushrooms - *100g (4oz) sliced*
Fresh single cream - *30ml (2 tbsp)*

METHOD

1 Skin the chicken and toss in seasoned flour. Melt butter in a frying pan and then fry chicken until golden. Drain and remove from the pan.

2 Add the onion and garlic to the pan and fry until golden.

3 Add the tomatoes, sugar, stock and chicken. Bring to the boil. Cover and simmer for 45 minutes. Add mushrooms and cook a further 15 minutes or until the chicken is tender. Stir in the cream just before serving.

365 Calories per portion Ⓕ

Beef & Horseradish Savoury SERVES 4

Minced beef - *450g (1lb)*
Onion - *1 small, finely chopped*
Creamed horseradish - *10ml (2 tsp)*
Fresh white breadcrumbs - *50g (2oz)*
Dried mixed herbs - *5ml (1 tsp)*
Salt *and freshly ground* **black pepper**
Egg - *1 (size 3) yolk*

Butter - *25g (1oz)*
Green pepper - *1 small, de-seeded and diced*
Plain flour - *25g (1 oz)*
Fresh milk - *300ml (½ pint)*
Canned tomatoes - *213g (7½ oz) can, chopped*

METHOD

1 Mix the minced beef, onion, 5ml (1 tsp) horseradish, breadcrumbs and mixed herbs. Season lightly and bind together with the egg yolk. Divide into 8 and shape into rissoles 6 x 2.5cm (2½ x 1 inch) on a floured board. Chill.

2 Melt the butter in a saucepan and gently fry the pepper for 2-3 minutes. Stir in the flour, remaining horseradish, milk and tomatoes. Season lightly, cover and simmer for 5 minutes.

3 Dry fry the rissoles in a frying pan for about 5 minutes on each side until browned and thoroughly cooked.
Serve the sauce separately.

---

455 Calories per portion Ⓕ

Cannelloni SERVES 4

Minced beef - *275g (10oz)*
Onion - *100g (4oz) finely chopped*
Garlic clove - *1, crushed*
Dried mixed herbs - *2.5ml (½ tsp)*
Salt *and freshly ground* **black pepper**
Canned tomatoes - *213g (7½ oz) can, chopped*
Mushrooms - *100g (4oz) sliced*
Bay leaf - *1*

Tomato purée - *10ml (2 tsp)*
Beef stock - *150ml (¼ pint)*
Dried lasagne - *8 sheets*
Plain flour - *25g (1oz)*
Butter - *25g (1oz)*
Fresh milk - *350ml (12 fl oz)*
English Cheddar cheese - *50g (2oz) finely grated*
Parsley - *for garnish*

METHOD

1 Dry fry the minced beef in a non-stick frying pan with the onion, garlic and mixed herbs until browned. Season and add the tomatoes, mushrooms, bay leaf, tomato purée and stock. Cover, bring almost to the boil and simmer for 30 minutes.

2 Cook the lasagne as directed on the packet. Divide the meat filling between the pasta sheets and roll up loosely. Place in the base of a greased ovenproof dish.

3 Place the flour, butter and milk in a saucepan. Heat stirring continuously until the sauce thickens and boils. Cook for one minute. Season lightly, remove from the heat and add the cheese.

4 Pour the sauce over the pasta and bake at 190°C (375°F), mark 5 for 25-30 minutes. Serve garnished with parsley.

640 Calories per portion Ⓕ

Macaroni Bake SERVES 4

Short cut macaroni - *175g (6oz)*
Minced beef - *350g (12oz)*
Onion - *1 small, chopped*
Salt *and freshly ground* **black pepper**
Canned tomatoes - *213g (7½ oz) can, chopped*
Dried mixed herbs - *2.5ml (½ tsp)*

Butter - *25g (1oz)*
Plain flour - *25g (1oz)*
Fresh milk - *450ml (¾ pint)*
Red Leicester cheese - *100g (4oz) finely grated*
Peanuts - *25g (1oz) roughly chopped*

METHOD

1 Cook macaroni according to the instructions on the packet. Drain well and place half in the base of an ovenproof dish.

2 Dry fry the mince in a non-stick frying pan with the onion until brown. Season lightly, add the tomatoes and herbs, bring just to the boil and simmer for 10 minutes.

3 Place butter, flour and milk in a saucepan, heat stirring continuously until the sauce thickens and boils. Cook for one minute. Remove from the heat, season lightly and add 75g (3oz) cheese.

4 Place the mince on top of the macaroni, followed by the remaining macaroni. Cover with the sauce and sprinkle with the remaining cheese and peanuts. Bake at 200°C (400°F), mark 6 for 20 minutes. Serve immediately.

---

520 Calories per portion Ⓕ

Marrow Moussaka SERVES 4

Minced beef - *450g (1lb)*
Onion - *1 small, chopped*
Dried oregano - *large pinch*
Plain flour - *40g (1½ oz)*
Beef stock - *150ml (¼ pint)*
Tomato purée - *10ml (2 tsp)*
Salt *and freshly ground* **black pepper**
Marrow - *1 medium sized*
Tomatoes - *225g (8oz) skinned and sliced*
Butter - *15g (½ oz)*
Fresh milk - *350ml (12 fl oz)*
Nutmeg - *2.5ml (½ tsp) grated*
English Cheddar cheese - *100g (4oz) grated*
Watercress and tomato - *for garnish*

in a greased 1.4 litre (2½ pint) ovenproof dish, finishing with a layer of marrow.

4 Place the remaining flour, butter and milk in a saucepan, heat stirring continuously until the sauce thickens and boils. Season lightly, remove from the heat and stir in the nutmeg and 75g (3oz) cheese. Pour sauce over the marrow and sprinkle with the remaining cheese.

5 Bake at 200°C (400°F), mark 6 for 20 minutes until golden. Garnish with watercress and tomato.

METHOD

1 Dry fry the mince in a non-stick frying pan with the onion and oregano until browned. Stir in 15g (½ oz) of flour, stock and tomato purée. Season lightly, bring almost to the boil, simmer for 15 minutes.

2 Skin the marrow, remove the seeds and cut into large cubes. Cook in boiling salted water for 5-10 minutes, until just tender. Drain well.

3 Layer the meat mixture, tomato slices and marrow

490 Calories per portion Ⓕ

Beef Cobbler SERVES 6

Lean stewing beef - *700g (1½ lb) cubed*
Plain flour - *25g (1oz), lightly seasoned*
Butter - *100g (4oz)*
Onion - *1 large, sliced*
Beef stock - *300ml (½ pint)*
Tomatoes - *4, skinned and quartered*

Self raising flour - *175g (6oz)*
Dried mixed herbs - *5ml (1 tsp)*
Fresh milk - *150ml (¼ pint)*

METHOD

1 Coat beef in the seasoned flour (shake in a plastic bag).

2 Melt half the butter in a large frying pan and fry the onion and beef until brown. Add the stock and tomatoes and pour into a casserole. Cover and cook at 150°C (300°F), mark 2 for 2½-3 hours until tender.

3 Sieve the self raising flour, a pinch of salt and the herbs into a bowl. Rub in the remaining butter. Mix to a soft dough with milk and knead lightly on a floured board. Cut into rounds with a 5cm (2inch) cutter.

4 Remove casserole from the oven and arrange rounds on top of the beef. Brush with a little milk and bake at 220°C (425°F), mark 7 for 10-15 minutes until golden.

515 Calories per portion

Father's Day Steak SERVES 4

Fillet, Rump or Sirloin steak - *4 x 175g (6oz) pieces, 2cm (¾ inch) thick*
Garlic cloves - *2, finely chopped*
Black pepper - *freshly ground*
Butter - *25g (1oz)*
Button mushrooms - *100g (4oz) thinly sliced*
Onion - *25g (1oz) finely chopped*
Fresh milk - *150ml (¼ pint) + 15ml (1 tbsp)*
Worcestershire sauce - *15ml (1 tbsp)*
Brandy - *15ml (1 tbsp)*
Cornflour - *15g (½ oz)*

Lemon juice - *15ml (1 tbsp)*
Fresh single or soured cream - *150ml (5 fl oz)*
Parsley - *15ml (1 tbsp) chopped*

METHOD

1 Rub steaks on both sides with garlic and black pepper and grill for between 2 and 7 minutes on each side according to taste. Keep warm.

2 Melt the butter in a saucepan and quickly fry the mushrooms and onion until tender. Add 150ml (¼ pint) milk, Worcestershire sauce and brandy.

3 Blend the cornflour with 15ml (1 tbsp) milk, add to the pan and bring to the boil. Season lightly.

4 Stir in the lemon juice, cream, and parsley. Reheat but do not boil and pour over the steaks. Serve immediately.

315 Calories per portion Ⓕ

Coconut Beef Curry SERVES 6

Natural yogurt - *150g (5oz) low fat*
Garlic clove - *1 crushed*
Curry powder - *15ml (1 tbsp)*
Lean stewing beef - *700g (1½ lb) cubed*
Fresh milk - *150ml (¼ pint)*
Desiccated coconut - *50g (2oz)*
Canned tomatoes - *400g (14oz) can*

Beef stock - *150ml (¼ pint)*
Cornflour - *25g (1oz)*
Boiled rice - *to serve*

METHOD

1 Blend the yogurt, garlic and curry powder and stir in the beef. Leave for at least one hour.

2 Pour hot milk over the coconut, cool quickly and refrigerate until needed.

3 Place beef and its marinade in a large saucepan. Add the coconut, milk, tomatoes and stock. Cover, bring almost to the boil and simmer for 2 hours or until tender.

4 Blend cornflour with a little milk, stir into the curry and heat until the sauce thickens and boils. Cook for one minute and serve with boiled rice.

---

460 Calories per portion

Family Beef Stroganoff SERVES 4

Stewing beef - *550g (1¼ lb) cubed*
Plain flour - *40g (1½ oz)*
Butter - *40g (1½ oz)*
Onion - *1 large, sliced*
Garlic clove - *1, crushed*
Mushrooms - *100g (4oz) sliced*
Beef stock - *300ml (½ pint)*
Tomato purée - *15ml (1 tbsp)*

Worcestershire sauce - *10ml (2 tsp)*
Salt - *2.5ml (½ tsp)*
Paprika - *2.5ml (½ tsp)*
Fresh soured cream - *150ml (5 fl oz)*

METHOD

1 Coat meat in the flour. Melt 25g (1oz) butter and cook meat until brown. Remove from the pan.

2 Fry the onion in remaining butter until soft. Add the garlic and mushrooms and cook for 2 minutes.

3 Blend in any remaining flour, then add stock, tomato purée, Worcestershire sauce, seasonings and meat. Heat, stirring continuously, until the sauce thickens and boils.

4 Cover the pan and simmer gently for 1½-2 hours, until the meat is tender.

5 Stir in most of the soured cream. Reheat but do not boil. Serve with pasta and trickle remaining cream over the top.

420 Calories per portion Ⓕ

Baked Lasagne SERVES 6

Streaky bacon - *75g (3oz) chopped*
Onion - *100g (4oz) chopped*
Carrot - *75g (3oz) chopped*
Celery - *1 stick, chopped*
Lean minced beef - *350g (12oz)*
Garlic cloves - *2, crushed*
Tomato purée - *30ml (2 tbsp)*
White wine - *90ml (6 tbsp)*

Canned chopped tomatoes - *425g (15oz) can*
Salt *and freshly ground* **black pepper**
Fresh single cream - *75ml (2½ fl oz)*
Lasagne sheets - *175g (6oz)*
English mozzarella - *225g (8oz) sliced*

METHOD

1 Gently fry the bacon, onion, carrot and celery in a large saucepan for 10 minutes until tender. Add the mince and fry until brown.

2 Stir in the garlic, tomato purée, wine and tomatoes. Season lightly. Bring to the boil and simmer for 40 minutes. Stir in the cream.

3 Cook the lasagne as directed on the packet. Place a layer in the base and around the edge of a greased ovenproof dish. Layer with meat sauce, Mozzarella and lasagne, finishing with a thick layer of Mozzarella.

4 Bake at 180°C (350°F), mark 4 for 30 minutes until the topping is golden. Serve immediately.

---

370 Calories per portion

Toreador Pancakes SERVES 4

Plain flour - *100g (4oz)*
Egg - *1 (size 3)*
Fresh milk - *300ml (½ pint)*
Butter - *15g (½ oz)*
Onion - *1 small, chopped*

Corned beef - *225g (8oz) cubed*
Condensed tomato soup - *300g (10½ oz) can*
Fresh white breadcrumbs - *40g (1½ oz) toasted*
or
Crushed crisps - *25g (1oz) packet*

METHOD

1 Sift the flour and a pinch of salt into a bowl. Make a well in the centre and break in the egg. Gradually add half the milk, beating to form a smooth batter. Stir in the remaining milk and beat well. Use a 20.5cm (8 inch) frying pan to make 8 pancakes.

2 Melt the butter and gently fry the onion. Add corned beef and heat gently. Use to fill the pancakes then place them in an ovenproof dish. Pour the undiluted soup over the pancakes, sprinkle with the breadcrumbs or crushed crisps and bake at 190°C (375°F), mark 5 for 15-20 minutes.

405 Calories per portion

Monday Pie   SERVES 4

Cold roast beef - *225g (8oz)*
Onion - *75g (3oz) chopped*
Canned tomatoes - *213g (7½ oz) drained*
Canned baked beans - *213g (7oz)*
Plain flour - *5ml (1 tsp)*
Gravy powder - *5ml (1 tsp)*
Salt *and freshly ground* **black pepper**
Potatoes - *550g (1¼ lb) sliced*
Butter - *10ml (2 tsp) melted*
English Cheddar cheese - *50g (2oz) grated*

METHOD

1 Mince roast beef and onion into a basin. Stir in tomatoes, baked beans, flour and gravy powder. Season lightly and turn into a 1 litre (1¾ pint) shallow ovenproof dish.

2 Peel and slice the potatoes. Arrange on top of the meat. Season and brush with melted butter. Bake at 190°C (375°F), mark 5 for 40 minutes, sprinkling with cheese after 30 minutes.

350 Calories per portion

Beef Layer Pie with Yogurt Topping

Onions - *100g (4oz) chopped*
Butter - *15g (½ oz)*
Cold roast beef - *225g (8oz) minced*
Dried mixed herbs - *2.5ml (½ tsp)*
Tomato purée - *30ml (2 tbsp)*
Worcestershire sauce - *5ml (2 tsp)*
Salt *and freshly ground* **black pepper**
Cooked potatoes - *450g (1lb) sliced*
Tomatoes - *225g (8oz) skinned and chopped*

Plain flour - *25g (1oz)*
Egg - *1 (size 3) beaten*
Natural yogurt - *150g (5oz) low fat*
Paprika - *for garnish*   SERVES 4

METHOD

1 Fry the onions gently in the butter. Add the meat, mixed herbs, tomato purée and Worcestershire sauce. Season lightly.

2 Arrange a layer of potato in the base of a 1 litre (1¾ pint) casserole dish, cover with the meat, followed by the tomatoes and finally the remaining potatoes. Cover and bake at 190°C (375°F), mark 5 for 20 minutes.

3 Blend the flour into the beaten egg and stir in the yogurt. Season lightly and spoon over the potato. Bake a further 30 minutes and serve dusted with paprika.

595 Calories per portion

Lamb Kebabs with Barbecue Sauce SERVES 4

Onion - *50g (2oz) finely chopped*
Butter - *25g (1oz)*
Worcestershire sauce - *15ml (1 tbsp)*
Tomato ketchup - *30ml (2 tbsp)*
Garlic clove - *1, finely chopped*
Lemon juice - *15ml (1 tbsp)*
Demerara sugar - *15ml (1 tbsp)*

Natural yogurt - *150g (5oz) low fat*
Black pepper - *freshly ground*
Shallots or baby onions - *8*
Lean shoulder or leg of lamb - *350g (12oz)*
Chipolata sausages - *225g (8oz)*
Button mushrooms - *8*
Tomatoes - *4 small, halved*
Long grain rice - *225g (8oz)*

METHOD

1 Fry the onion in butter in a saucepan until soft. Remove pan from heat and stir in Worcestershire sauce, ketchup, garlic, lemon juice, sugar and yogurt. Season lightly. Divide the sauce in half.

2 Place shallots in boiling water for one minute. Cube the lamb and twist the sausages into bite sized pieces. Thread the lamb, sausages, onion, mushrooms and tomatoes onto skewers.

3 Brush the kebabs liberally with half the sauce. Cook under a pre-heated grill, turning frequently brushing with sauce until the meat is tender.

4 Cook rice according to instructions on packet.

5 Gently heat the remaining sauce, do not allow it to boil. Serve kebabs on rice, serve sauce separately.

405 Calories per portion

Crispy Lamb Bake SERVES 4

Butter - *25g (1oz)*
Curry powder - *10ml (2 tsp)*
Fresh milk - *300ml (½ pint)*
Plain flour - *25g (1oz)*
Cooked lamb - *225g (8oz) diced*
Parsley - *15ml (1 tbsp) chopped*
Salt *and freshly ground* **black pepper**

Potatoes - *450g (1lb)*
English Cheddar cheese - *25g (1oz) finely grated*
Potato crisps - *1 packet, low fat*
Tomato - *for garnish*

METHOD

1 Melt the butter in a saucepan, add curry powder and cook for 2 minutes. Add the milk and flour, heat stirring continuously until the sauce thickens and boils. Cook for one minute.

2 Stir in the lamb and parsley, season lightly and pour into a 1 litre (1¾ pint) ovenproof dish.

3 Cook potatoes, mash with a little butter and milk and spread over the lamb. Sprinkle with cheese and crushed crisps. Bake at 190°C (375°F), mark 5 for 20 minutes. Serve garnished with tomato.

600 Calories per portion Ⓕ

Sweet & Sour Lamb SERVES 4

Lamb cutlets - *8 x 100g (4oz) each*
Onion - *1 small, chopped*
Butter - *5ml (1 tsp)*
Cornflour - *30ml (2 tbsp)*
Vinegar - *30ml (2 tbsp)*
Soy sauce - *5ml (1 tsp)*
Fresh milk - *150ml (¼ pint)*
Pineapple rings - *439g (15½ oz) can*
Chicken stock cube - *1*
Glacé cherries - *4 for garnish*

METHOD

1 Grill the cutlets on both sides until golden.

2 Gently fry the onion in the butter in a large saucepan until soft.

3 Blend the cornflour with the vinegar then add the soy sauce, milk, drained pineapple juice and crumbled stock cube. Add to the onions and bring to the boil, stirring continuously. Add the cutlets and simmer for 10 minutes. Serve garnished with pineapple rings and cherries.

430 Calories per portion Ⓕ

Kufta with Tomato Sauce SERVES 4

Onion - *1 large, finely chopped*
Minced lamb - *225g (8oz)*
Minced beef - *225g (8oz)*
Wholemeal breadcrumbs - *90g (3½ oz)*
Dried oregano - *2.5ml (½ tsp)*
Fresh parsley - *15-30ml (1-2 tbsp) chopped*
Fresh milk - *150ml (¼ pint)*
Cayenne pepper - *large pinch*
Salt *and freshly ground* **pepper**

SAUCE
Canned tomatoes - *213g (7½ oz) can, chopped*
Plain flour - *25g (1oz)*
Fresh milk - *300ml (½ pint)*
Creamed horseradish - *5ml-10ml (1-2 tsp)*
Black pepper - *freshly ground*

METHOD

1 Mix the onion, lamb, beef, 40g (1½ oz) breadcrumbs, herbs, milk and seasonings.

2 Shape the mixture into 8 patties (kufta) and coat with the remaining breadcrumbs. Grill gently for 5-10 minutes on each side or until cooked through.

3 Blend the tomatoes and flour in a saucepan. Add the milk and creamed horseradish. Season with pepper. Heat, stirring continuously, until the sauce thickens and boils. Cook for one minute. Serve with the kufta.

460 Calories per portion

Cheshire Lamb Crumble SERVES 4

Cooked lamb - *350g (12oz)*
Onion - *1 medium, chopped*
Plain flour - *115g (4½ oz)*
Tomato purée - *15ml (1 tbsp)*
Beef stock - *300ml (½ pint)*
Salt *and freshly ground* **black pepper**
Butter - *50g (2oz)*
Cheshire cheese - *50g (2oz) grated*
Dried mixed herbs - *2.5ml (½ tsp)*

METHOD

1 Mince the lamb and onion together. Stir in
15g (½ oz) flour, the tomato purée and stock.
Season lightly. Turn into a shallow, greased
ovenproof dish.

2 Rub the butter into the remaining flour until the
mixture resembles fine breadcrumbs. Stir in the
cheese and herbs. Season lightly and sprinkle over
the meat. Bake at 190°C (375°F), mark 5 for
45-60 minutes until golden. Serve immediately.

515 Calories per portion

Piquant Lamb Chops SERVES 4

Best end lamb cutlets - *8 x 100g (4oz) each*
Onion sauce mix - *1 packet*
Fresh milk - *300ml (½ pint)*
Capers - *15ml (1 tbsp)*
Gherkins - *2, sliced*
Stuffed olives - *for garnish*

METHOD

1 Grill the cutlets on both sides until golden and
cooked according to taste.

2 Make up the sauce mix with the milk as
directed on the packet.
Stir in the capers and gherkins.

3 Serve the cutlets coated with a little sauce
and garnished with stuffed olives.
Serve remaining sauce separately.

405 Calories per portion

Greek Shepherd's Pie SERVES 6

Long grain rice - *175g (6oz)*
Butter - *25g (1oz)*
Plain flour - *50g (2oz)*
Fresh milk - *300ml (½ pint)*
Onion - *1 large, chopped*
Egg - *1 (size 3) beaten*
English Cheddar cheese - *100g (4oz) grated*
Salt *and freshly ground* **black pepper**
Cooked lamb - *275g (10oz) minced*

Beef stock - *150ml (¼ pint)*
Tomato ketchup - *30ml (2 tbsp)*
Tomato and onion - *for garnish*

METHOD

1 Cook rice according to instructions on the packet.

2 Put butter, flour and milk in a saucepan and heat, stirring continuously until the sauce thickens and boils. Cook for one minute. Add half the onion, the egg, rice and 75g (3oz) cheese. Season lightly.

3 Mix the lamb with the stock, ketchup and remaining onion and season lightly.

4 Place half the rice mixture in a greased ovenproof dish, cover with the lamb then top with the remaining rice. Sprinkle with 25g (1oz) cheese and bake at 190°C (375°F), mark 5 for 45 minutes. Serve garnished with tomato and onion.

---

395 Calories per portion Ⓕ

Moussaka SERVES 6

Aubergine - *3 medium, sliced 1cm (½ inch) thick*
Olive oil - *45-60ml (3-4 tbsp)*
Butter - *40g (1½ oz)*
Onion - *100g (4oz) chopped*
Garlic clove - *1, finely chopped*
Cooked lamb - *450g (1 lb) minced*
Canned tomatoes - *400g (14oz) chopped*
Salt *and freshly ground* **black pepper**

Plain flour - *25g (1oz)*
Fresh milk - *300ml (½ pint)*
English Cheddar cheese - *75g (3oz) grated*

METHOD

1 Place the aubergines in a colander, sprinkle with salt, cover and leave to drain for ½ hour. Dry well on kitchen paper then fry in the oil until soft. Place in the base of a shallow 1.7 litre (3 pint) ovenproof dish.

2 Melt 15g (½ oz) butter in a saucepan and gently fry the onion. Add garlic, lamb and tomatoes, season lightly and arrange over the aubergines.

3 Place the flour, remaining butter and milk in a saucepan, heat stirring continuously until the sauce thickens and boils. Remove from the heat, add the cheese and pour over the meat. Bake at 190°C (375°F), mark 5 for 30 minutes.

500 Calories per portion

Pork Kebabs with Mustard Sauce SERVES 4

Long grain rice - *225g (8oz)*
Canned sweetcorn - *198g (7oz) drained*
Parsley - *30ml (2 tbsp) chopped*
Pork fillet - *350g (12oz) cubed*
Tomatoes - *8 small, halved*
Button mushrooms - *16*
Salt *and freshly ground* black pepper

Butter - *melted, for brushing the kebabs*
Butter - *15g (½ oz)*
Plain flour - *25g (1oz)*
Fresh milk - *300ml (½ pint)*
Dry mustard - *10ml (2 tsp)*
Vinegar - *10ml (2 tsp)*

METHOD

1 Cook the rice according to the instructions on the packet. Heat the corn and stir into the rice with the parsley. Keep warm.

2 Thread the pork, tomatoes and mushrooms onto skewers. Season and brush with melted butter. Cook under a pre-heated grill until the meat is tender.

3 Place the butter, flour and milk in a saucepan, heat, stirring continuously until the sauce thickens and boils. Cook for one minute. Blend mustard and vinegar and add to the sauce. Season lightly and simmer for 1 minute.

4 Serve kebabs on the prepared rice and serve the sauce separately.

---

340 Calories per portion **F**

Pork & Apple Casserole SERVES 4

Butter - *25g (1oz)*
Pork tenderloin - *350g (12oz) cubed*
Onion - *1 large, sliced*
Plain flour - *50g (2oz)*
Fresh milk - *300ml (½ pint)*
Dry cider - *300ml (½ pint)*
Dried thyme - *generous pinch*
Dried sage - *generous pinch*
Salt *and freshly ground* black pepper
Cooking apples - *350g (12oz) peeled and sliced*
Fresh single cream - *30ml (2 tbsp)*

METHOD

1 Melt the butter in a large saucepan and fry the pork until brown. Using a draining spoon, remove pork and place in a casserole dish.

2 Add the onion to the pan and fry until soft. Stir in the flour and cook for 1 minute. Gradually stir in the milk and cider and heat, stirring continuously until the sauce thickens and boils. Add herbs, season lightly and pour over the pork. Cover and bake at 180°C (350°F), mark 4 for 1 hour.

3 Remove casserole from the oven and stir in the apple. Return to the oven for 30 minutes or until the pork is tender. Stir in the cream before serving.

545 Calories per portion Ⓕ

Kentish Pork SERVES 4

Pork loin chops - *4 x 200g (7oz) each*
Onion - *1 small, chopped*
Butter - *40g (1½ oz)*
Plain flour - *25g (1oz)*
Salt *and freshly ground* **black pepper**
Chicken stock - *150ml (¼ pint)*
Fresh milk - *150ml (¼ pint)*
Cooking apples - *350g (12oz) peeled and cored*
Parsley - *chopped for garnish*

METHOD

1 Grill chops on both sides until cooked through.

2 Gently fry the onion in 25g (1oz) butter in a large saucepan until soft. Add the flour, season and cook for 1 minute. Gradually blend in the stock and milk, heat stirring continuously until the sauce thickens and boils.

3 Chop half the apple, add to the sauce along with the chops and simmer for 15 minutes. Transfer to a serving dish and keep warm.

4 Slice the remaining apple, sauté in the remaining butter and use to garnish the chops. Serve sprinkled with parsley.

---

570 Calories per portion

Saucy Pork SERVES 4

Fresh milk - *150ml (¼ pint)*
Sage and onion stuffing mix - *25g (1oz)*
Minced pork - *450g (1lb)*
Onion - *1 small, grated*
Plain flour - *100g (4oz)*
Egg - *1 (size 3)*
Salt *and freshly ground* **black pepper**
Oil - *5ml (1 tsp) for frying*

SAUCE
Onion - *½ small, chopped*
Green pepper - *1 small, cored and de-seeded*
Red pepper - *1 small, cored and de-seeded*
Butter - *15g (½ oz)*
Canned pineapple pieces - *225g (8oz) can, drained*
Soy sauce - *15ml (1 tbsp)*
Vinegar - *30ml (2 tbsp)*
Sugar - *15ml (1 tbsp)*
Cornflour - *15ml (1 tbsp)*

METHOD

1 Heat the milk to boiling, pour onto the stuffing mix and stand for 10 minutes.

2 Mix the pork, onion, flour, egg and stuffing. Season lightly, beat well then divide into 8. Shape into patties and fry in oil in a non-stick pan for about 5 minutes on each side. Drain on kitchen paper.

3 Fry the onion and thinly sliced peppers in the butter for 2-3 minutes. Add the pineapple, 45ml (3 tbsp) of the pineapple juice, soy sauce, vinegar and sugar.

4 Blend the cornflour with 60ml (4 tbsp) water, add to the sauce and bring almost to the boil. Add patties and simmer for 5 minutes before serving.

495 Calories per portion Ⓕ

Somerset Pork Chops SERVES 4

Pork chops - *4 x 175g (6oz)*
Butter - *25g (1oz)*
Onion - *175g (6oz) sliced*
Plain flour - *25g (1oz)*
Dry cider - *150ml (¼ pint)*
Dried sage - *5ml (1 tsp)*
Salt *and freshly ground* **black pepper**
Fresh single cream - *30ml (2 tbsp)*

METHOD

1 Dry fry or grill the chops until the fat is golden brown. Arrange drained chops in an ovenproof dish.

2 Melt the butter in a saucepan, fry the onion until soft then stir in the flour.

3 Gradually add the cider, 60ml (4 tbsp) water and sage. Season lightly. Pour over the chops. Bake at 190°C (375°F), mark 5 for 30-40 minutes. Serve with the cream drizzled over the top.

320 Calories per portion Ⓕ

Curried Pork SERVES 4

Pork fillet - *350g (12oz) diced*
Plain flour - *40g (1½ oz)*
Curry powder - *10ml (2 tsp)*
Butter - *25g (1oz)*
Onion - *100g (4oz) chopped*
Celery - *2 sticks, chopped*
Fresh milk - *450ml (¾ pint)*
Sultanas - *50g (2oz)*
Cauliflower florets - *225g (8oz)*

METHOD

1 Toss the pork in a mixture of flour and curry powder. Fry in the butter until brown.

2 Add the onion and celery and fry until soft. Stir in any remaining flour and curry powder.

3 Slowly add the milk, stirring continuously. Add the sultanas and cauliflower, cover and simmer for 20 minutes. Serve on a bed of rice.

390 Calories per portion

Crispy Cheese Flan SERVES 6

Plain flour - *175g (6oz)*
Butter - *75g (3oz) diced*
English Cheddar cheese - *175g (5oz) grated*
Bacon - *75g (3oz) dry fried until just golden*
Eggs - *2 (size 3) separated*
Salt *and freshly ground* **black pepper**
Fresh milk - *150ml (¼ pint)*
Parsley - *chopped for garnish*

METHOD

1 Place flour and a pinch of salt in a bowl.
Rub in the butter until the mixture resembles fine
breadcrumbs. Add about 30ml (2 tbsp) water and
mix to a dough. Knead lightly. Roll out on a
floured surface and line a 20cm (8 inch) flan ring.

2 Mix 100g (4oz) cheese, the bacon, egg yolks
and milk. Season lightly, pour into the pastry
case and bake at 190°C (375°F), mark 5 for
20 minutes or until set.

3 Whisk the egg whites until stiff, fold in the
remaining cheese and spread over the flan.
Bake a further 10-15 minutes until golden
and serve sprinkled with parsley.

---

500 Calories per portion

Savoury Suet Roll SERVES 6

Self raising flour - *225g (8oz)*
Suet - *100g (4oz)*
Fresh mixed herbs - *5ml (1 tsp) chopped (optional)*
Fresh milk - *150ml (¼ pint)*
Yeast extract - *to taste*
Streaky bacon - *225g (8oz) chopped*
Onion - *1 small, chopped*
Red Leicester cheese - *175g (6oz) grated*
Parsley - *10ml (2 tsp) chopped*
Tomato - *for garnish*

METHOD

1 Mix the flour, suet, herbs and a pinch of salt.
Gradually add the milk and mix to form a soft dough.
Leave to stand for 5 minutes. Roll out on a floured board
to a rectangle 37.5 x 30cm (15 x 12 inch). Using a hot
knife, thinly spread yeast extract over the dough.

2 Dry fry the bacon and onion until golden.
Drain well and sprinkle over the dough,
followed by the cheese and parsley.

3 Roll up like a Swiss roll, place on a piece of
greased foil and over wrap loosely. Bake at
200°C (400°F), mark 6 for 30 minutes. Open foil and
bake a further 15 minutes until golden. Serve immediately.

Pork & Ham

440 Calories per portion

Cauliflower Crisp   SERVES 4

Cauliflower - *1 whole*
Butter - *25g (1oz)*
Button mushrooms - *175g (6oz) sliced*
Plain flour - *40g (1½ oz)*
Fresh milk - *450ml (¾ pint)*

Salt *and freshly ground* black pepper
Streaky bacon - *175g (6oz) grilled and chopped*
English Cheddar cheese - *100g (4oz) grated*
Fresh wholemeal breadcrumbs - *30ml (2 tbsp)*
Parsley - *for garnish*

METHOD

1 Cook the cauliflower in boiling salted water until tender.
Drain and place in a round casserole dish.

2 Melt the butter in a saucepan and gently fry the
mushrooms for 3 minutes. Add the flour and milk then
heat, stirring continuously until the sauce thickens
and boils. Cook for one minute. Remove from the heat,
season lightly and add bacon and 75g (3oz) cheese.
Pour the sauce over the cauliflower.

3 Mix remaining cheese and breadcrumbs, sprinkle
over the sauce and brown under a hot grill.
Serve garnished with parsley.

230 Calories per portion Ⓕ

Celery au Gratin   SERVES 4

Canned celery hearts - *450g (1lb) can, drained*
Cooked ham - *4 x 25g (1oz) slices*
Butter - *15g (½ oz)*
Plain flour - *25g (1oz)*
Fresh milk - *300ml (½ pint)*
Salt *and freshly ground* black pepper
English Cheddar cheese - *100g (4oz)*
Fresh white breadcrumbs - *30ml (2 tbsp)*

METHOD

1 Divide the celery hearts into 4 portions and wrap
a slice of ham around each. Place in a greased shallow
ovenproof dish.

2 Place the butter, flour and milk in a saucepan,
heat stirring until the sauce thickens and boils.
Cook for one minute. Remove from the heat,
season to taste and stir in half the cheese.
Pour the sauce over the celery.

3 Mix breadcrumbs and remaining cheese
together, sprinkle over the sauce and bake at
200°C (400°F), mark 6 for 30 minutes until golden.

TIP: You can use celery or cooked leeks instead of
in this recipe.

375 Calories per portion Ⓕ

Leek Pie SERVES 6

Plain flour - *175g (6oz)*
Butter - *75g (3oz) diced*
Caerphilly cheese - *75g (3oz) finely grated*
Eggs - *3 (size 3)*
Fresh milk - *105ml (7 tbsp)*

Leeks - *450g (1lb) cut in 2.5cm (1 inch) slices*
Cooked ham or bacon - *175g (6oz) chopped*
Salt *and freshly ground* **black pepper**

METHOD

1 Sieve flour into a bowl, rub in the butter until it resembles fine breadcrumbs. Stir in the cheese. Add one egg, beaten with 45ml (3 tbsp) milk and mix to a soft dough. Use two thirds to line a 27.5 x 17.5cm (11 x 7 inch) shallow tin.

2 Par-boil the leeks in salted water for 5 minutes. Drain well.

3 Sprinkle the ham in the base of the tin. Beat remaining eggs and milk, season lightly and pour over the ham. Cover with sliced leeks.

4 Cover the pie with the remaining pastry and brush with milk. Bake at 200°C (400°F), mark 6 for 15 minutes then at 180°C (350°F), mark 4 for 25 minutes or until golden. Serve hot or cold.

---

410 Calories per portion

Stuffed Peppers SERVES 4

Red or green peppers - *4 large*
Butter - *15g (½ oz)*
Onion - *100g (4oz) chopped*
Cooked ham or bacon - *175g (6oz) diced*
Cooked rice - *175g (6oz)*
Soy sauce - *45ml (3 tbsp)*
English Cheddar cheese - *50g (2oz) grated*
Chicken stock - *150ml (¼ pint)*

SAUCE
Butter - *15g (½ oz)*
Plain flour - *25g (1oz)*
Fresh milk - *300ml (½ pint)*
Made mustard - *5ml (1 tsp)*
Salt *and freshly ground* **black pepper**
English Cheddar cheese -
50g (2oz) grated

METHOD

1 Cut the tops off the peppers, remove cores and seeds. Blanch for 5 minutes and drain well.

2 Melt the butter in a saucepan and gently fry the onion. Add the ham, rice and soy sauce. Fill the peppers with this mixture and sprinkle with 50g (2oz) cheese. Stand in a casserole dish, small enough to prevent them falling over. Pour in the stock. Cover and cook at 190°C (375°F), mark 5 for about 30 minutes or until tender.

3 Place butter, flour and milk in a saucepan, heat stirring continuously until the sauce thickens and boils. Cook for one minute. Remove from the heat, season lightly and add the mustard and remaining cheese. Serve with the peppers.

595 Calories per portion Ⓕ

Sausage Goulash   SERVES 4

Pork sausages - *450g (1lb)*
Green pepper - *1 large, de-seeded*
Butter - *15g (½ oz)*
Onion - *1 small, chopped*
Garlic clove - *1, crushed (optional)*
Plain flour - *15ml (1 tbsp)*
Tomatoes - *225g (8oz) skinned and chopped*
Tomato purée - *15ml (1 tbsp)*
Paprika pepper - *15ml (1 tbsp)*

Condensed tomato soup - *300g (10.6oz) can*
Fresh milk - *300ml (½ pint)*
Potatoes - *450g (1lb) peeled and quartered*
Black pepper - *freshly ground*
Natural yogurt - *30ml (2 tbsp)*

METHOD

1 Grill sausages, cut in half and keep warm. Cut
3 slices from the pepper for garnish and dice the rest.

2 Melt the butter in a large saucepan and gently
fry the onion, garlic and diced green pepper for
5 minutes. Stir in the flour and cook for 2 minutes.

3 Stir in the tomatoes, tomato purée, paprika, soup,
milk, sausages and potatoes. Season with black pepper.
Cover and simmer for 20 minutes or
until potatoes are tender.
Serve garnished with yogurt and pepper.

---

615 Calories per portion Ⓕ

Sausage Stretcher   SERVES 4

Pork sausages - *350g (12oz)*
Macaroni or pasta shapes - *175g (6oz)*
Butter - *15g (½ oz)*
Button mushrooms - *100g (4oz)*
Leeks - *2, washed and sliced*
Canned sweetcorn - *198g (7oz) can, drained*
Condensed mushroom soup - *300g (10.6oz) can*
Fresh milk - *300ml (½ pint)*
Plain flour - *25g (1oz)*
Red Leicester cheese - *50g (2oz) grated*
Fresh white breadcrumbs - *30ml (2 tbsp)*
Tomato - *for garnish*

METHOD

1 Grill the sausages and cut in half. Keep warm.

2 Cook the pasta according to the directions on
the packet.

3 Melt the butter and gently cook the mushrooms
and leeks until tender. Stir in the sweetcorn.

4 Blend the soup and milk in a saucepan, whisk in the flour
and heat stirring continuously until boiling. Stir in the sausages,
pasta, mushrooms and leeks and heat through thoroughly. Transfer to
an ovenproof dish. Sprinkle with a mixture of cheese and breadcrumbs and
grill until golden. Serve garnished with tomato.

550 Calories per portion

Swede & Bacon Flan SERVES 4

PASTRY
Plain flour - *175g (6oz)*
Salt - *pinch*
Butter - *75g (3oz) diced*
Fresh milk - *30ml (2 tbsp)*

FILLING
Swede - *1 medium, peeled and diced*
Fresh milk - *300ml (½ pint)*
Plain flour - *25g (1oz)*
Butter - *15g (½ oz)*
Salt *and freshly ground* **black pepper**

Grated nutmeg - *large pinch*
Streaky bacon - *175g (6oz) chopped*
Onion - *1 small, finely chopped*
Watercress - *for garnish*

METHOD

1 Sift the flour and salt in a bowl. Rub in the butter until the mixture resembles fine breadcrumbs. Add 30ml (2 tbsp) milk and mix to a dough. Knead lightly and roll out on a floured board to line a 20.5cm (8 inch) flan ring.

2 Cook the swede in boiling salted water until just tender.

3 Place the milk, flour and butter in a saucepan and heat, stirring continuously until the sauce thickens and boils. Season lightly, add nutmeg and cook for one minute.

4 Dry fry 100g (4oz) of the bacon with the onion until golden and add to the sauce with the swede. Turn into the flan case and arrange strips of the remaining bacon over the top in a lattice pattern. Bake at 200°C (400°F), mark 6 for 30 minutes. Garnish with watercress.

---

500 Calories per portion

Frying Pan Pizza SERVES 4

BASE
Plain flour - *175g (6oz)*
Salt - *pinch*
Butter - *50g (2oz)*
Fresh milk - *150ml (¼ pint)*

TOPPING
Streaky bacon - *100g (4oz) chopped*
Onion - *1 small, sliced*
Tomatoes - *2, skinned and chopped*
Tomato chutney - *45ml (3 tbsp)*
Dried mixed herbs or oregano - *2.5ml (½ tsp)*
English Cheddar cheese - *100g (4oz) grated*
Parsley and tomato - *for garnish*

METHOD

1 Sift flour and salt into a bowl. Rub in 40g (1½ oz) butter until mixture resembles fine breadcrumbs. Add enough milk to mix to a dough. Shape into a round and roll out to fit a 20.5cm (8 inch) frying pan. Melt the remaining butter in the frying pan and fry the dough on one side until golden brown.

2 Dry fry the bacon and onion gently until golden then add the tomatoes, chutney and herbs. Season lightly and cook for 2 minutes.

3 Turn over the pizza base, spread with the tomato mixture and sprinkle with cheese. Cover and cook gently for 15-20 minutes. To give a golden topping, brown under a hot grill for a few minutes then garnish with tomato slices and grill a few minutes longer. Serve garnished with parsley.

340 Calories per portion

Ham & Pineapple Top Knots SERVES 4

Ham steaks - *4 round*
Crumpets - *4*
Mustard powder - *2.5ml (½ tsp)*
Fresh milk - *45ml (3 tbsp)*
English Cheddar cheese - *100g (4oz) grated*
Pineapple rings - *4*
Watercress - *for garnish*

METHOD

1 Gently grill the ham steaks and keep warm. Toast the crumpets.

2 Mix the mustard to a paste with a little milk. Add the rest of the milk and cheese. Spread this mixture over the crumpets and grill until golden.

3 Place a ham steak on each crumpet, top with a pineapple ring and heat thoroughly under a medium grill. Garnish with watercress.

305 Calories per portion Ⓕ

Savoury Meat Loaf SERVES 4

Streaky bacon - *175g (6oz) de-rinded*
Cooked ham or pork - *225g (8oz) minced*
Bread sauce mix - *40g (1½ oz) packet*
Cornflakes - *15g (½ oz) crumbled*
Onion - *25g (1oz) chopped*
Dried mixed herbs - *2.5ml (½ tsp)*
Tomato purée - *15ml (1 tbsp)*
Egg - *1 (size 3) beaten*
Fresh milk - *150ml (¼ pint)*
Salt *and freshly ground* **black pepper**

METHOD

1 Stretch the rashers of bacon with the back of a knife and use to line a 450g (1lb) loaf tin.

2 Mix the minced meat, bread sauce mix, cornflakes, onion, herbs and tomato purée.

3 Beat egg and milk, season lightly and stir into the meat mixture. Beat well and turn into the loaf tin. Cover the surface with foil and bake at 200°C (400°F), mark 6 for 1-1¼ hours. Cool for 15 minutes in the tin then turn out and serve hot with vegetables.

Alternatively: Cool quickly in the tin, chill for several hours in the refrigerator then turn out and serve with salad.

385 Calories per portion

Gala Ham Salad SERVES 6

Fresh milk - *450ml (¾ pint)*
Butter - *25g (1oz)*
Plain flour - *40g (1½ oz)*
Made mustard - *5ml (1 tsp)*
Dried mixed herbs - *large pinch*
Salt *and freshly ground* **black pepper**
Canned pineapple pieces - *425g (15oz) fruit and juice*

Lemon juice - *5ml (1tsp)*
Fresh single cream - *150ml (5 fl oz)*
Cooked ham - *450g (1lb) thickly sliced and cubed*
Celery - *4 sticks, chopped*
Tomatoes - *225g (8oz) skinned and chopped*
Egg noodles - *100g (4oz) cooked and cooled*
Parsley - *to garnish*

METHOD

1 Place milk, butter and flour in a saucepan, heat stirring continuously until the sauce thickens and boils. Add the mustard and herbs, season lightly and cook for 2 minutes. Pour into a large bowl and stir in most of the pineapple juice. Pour remaining juice over the surface but do not stir in. Cover and cool in the refrigerator.

2 Stir the lemon juice into the cream and leave for 5 minutes.

3 Stir the pineapple juice into the sauce. Add the cream, cubes of ham, celery, tomatoes, noodles and most of the pineapple pieces. Chill.

4 Pile the mixture on a bed of lettuce and serve garnished with pieces of pineapple and parsley.

---

340 Calories per portion

Ham & Banana Rolls SERVES 4

Fresh milk - *300ml (½ pint)*
Plain flour - *25g (1oz)*
Butter - *15g (½ oz)*
Salt *and freshly ground* **black pepper**
English Cheddar cheese - *150g (5oz) grated*
Cooked ham - *4 slices*
Made mustard - *to taste*
Bananas - *4 medium, peeled*
Parsley - *for garnish*

METHOD

1 Place milk, flour and butter in a saucepan and heat, stirring continuously until the sauce thickens and boils. Season lightly and cook for one minute. Remove from the heat and stir in 75g (3oz) of the cheese.

2 Spread each slice of ham with mustard. Wrap a slice of ham around each banana and place in a greased ovenproof dish. Pour sauce over the bananas and sprinkle with the remaining cheese. Bake at 180°C (350°F), mark 4 for 30 minutes until golden. Serve garnished with parsley.

Offal

360 Calories per portion Ⓕ

Italian Liver SERVES 4

Lambs or ox liver - *350g (12oz) cut in 2.5cm (1 inch) pieces*
Fresh milk - *300ml (½ pint)*
Plain flour - *25g (1oz)*
Salt *and freshly ground* **black pepper**
Butter - *40g (1½ oz)*
Onions - *450g (1lb) thinly sliced*
Beef stock - *150ml (¼ pint)*
Tomato purée - *30ml (2 tbsp)*
Garlic clove - *1, finely chopped*
Dried mixed herbs - *large pinch*
Fresh single cream - *30ml (2 tbsp)*
Parsley - *chopped for garnish*

METHOD

1 Soak the liver in the milk for one hour if using ox liver. Drain.

2 Season the flour and use to coat the liver. Melt half the butter in a frying pan and fry the liver until lightly browned. Drain the liver well and transfer to a plate.

3 Add the remaining butter and onions to the frying pan. Cook slowly until tender.

4 Gradually add the stock, milk, tomato purée, garlic and herbs. Heat, stirring continuously until the sauce thickens and boils. Season lightly, add the liver and simmer gently for 10-15 minutes. Trickle cream over the liver and garnish with parsley before serving.

---

355 Calories per portion Ⓕ

Savoury Liver Special SERVES 4

Salt *and freshly ground* **black pepper**
Plain flour - *50g (2oz)*
Lambs liver - *350g (12oz) sliced*
Butter - *40g (1½ oz)*
Mustard powder - *5ml (1 tsp)*
Paprika pepper - *5ml (1 tsp)*
Onion - *100g (4oz) chopped*
Fresh milk - *300ml (½ pint)*
Natural yogurt - *150g (5oz) low fat*

METHOD

1 Season 25g (1oz) of the flour and use to coat the liver. Gently fry in 25g (1oz) butter until cooked according to taste. Remove from the pan and keep warm.

2 Melt the remaining butter in a saucepan, add the mustard and paprika and cook for one minute. Add the onion and cook until soft.

3 Add the remaining flour and milk. Heat, stirring continuously until the sauce thickens and boils. Season lightly and cook for one minute. Remove from the heat and stir in the yogurt. Serve the paprika sauce poured over the liver.

340 Calories per portion Ⓕ

Spicy Lambs Liver SERVES 4

Plain flour - *50g (2oz)*
Cinnamon - *2.5ml (½ tsp)*
Mixed spice - *5ml (1 tsp)*
Salt *and freshly ground* **black pepper**
Lambs liver - *350g (12oz) cut into strips*
Butter - *40g (1½ oz)*
Onions - *2 medium, sliced*
Button mushrooms - *50g (2oz) sliced*
Beef stock - *150ml (¼ pint)*
Fresh milk - *150ml (¼ pint)*
Tomato ketchup - *15ml (1 tbsp)*
Worcestershire sauce - *15ml (1 tbsp)*

METHOD

1 Mix 25g (1oz) flour, cinnamon and mixed spice, season lightly and use to coat the liver.
2 Melt 15g (½ oz) butter in a frying pan and fry the onions until soft.
3 Add the remaining butter and gently fry the liver and mushrooms for 10 minutes.
4 Stir in any remaining flour then the stock, milk, ketchup and Worcestershire sauce. Heat, stirring continuously until the sauce thickens and boils. Cook for one minute. Serve immediately.

370 Calories per portion

Peanut Liver Casserole SERVES 4

Onion - *1 medium, sliced*
Beef stock - *150ml (¼ pint)*
Lambs liver - *450g (1lb) cut into strips*
Salt *and freshly ground* **black pepper**
Plain flour - *25g (1oz)*
Chilli powder - *2.5ml (½ tsp)*
Soy sauce - *15ml (1 tbsp)*
Tomato purée - *15ml (1 tbsp)*
Fresh milk - *300ml (½ pint)*
Roasted peanuts - *50g (2oz) for garnish*
Parsley - *chopped for garnish*

METHOD

1 Add the onion to the stock. Bring to the boil and simmer for 5 minutes.

2 Lightly season the flour and add the chilli powder. Coat the liver in the seasoned flour. Add to the stock and simmer for 2 minutes.

3 Add the soy sauce, tomato purée and milk. Cover and simmer for 5 minutes. Serve sprinkled with peanuts and parsley.

350 Calories per portion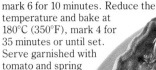

Liver Sausage Quiche   SERVES 6

PASTRY
Plain flour - *175g (6oz)*
Pinch of salt
Butter - *75g (3oz)*
Fresh milk - *30ml (2 tbsp)*
FILLING
Streaky bacon - *2 rashers, chopped*
Onion - *1 small, chopped*
Smooth liver sausage - *75g (3oz)*
Eggs - *2 (size 3)*
Fresh milk - *300ml (½ pint)*
English Cheddar cheese - *25g (1oz)*
Salt *and freshly ground* **black pepper**
Tomato slices and spring onion - *for garnish*

METHOD

1 Place flour and salt in a bowl. Rub in the butter until the mixture resembles fine breadcrumbs. Add the milk and mix to a dough. Knead lightly and roll out to line a 20.5cm (8 inch) flan ring. Bake 'blind' at 190°C (375°F), mark 5 for 20 minutes.

2 Lightly dry fry the bacon and onion until golden. Remove the skin from the liver sausage and cut into small cubes. Place all three ingredients in the base of the flan.

3 Beat the eggs with the milk, add the cheese, season lightly and pour into the flan case. Bake at 200°C (400°F), mark 6 for 10 minutes. Reduce the temperature and bake at 180°C (350°F), mark 4 for 35 minutes or until set. Serve garnished with tomato and spring onions.

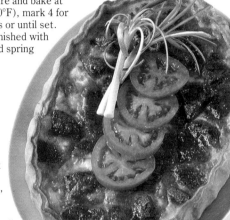

405 Calories per portion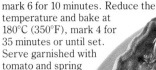

Hungry Hotpot   SERVES 4

Onions - *225g (8oz) sliced*
Butter - *25g (1oz)*
Lambs liver - *450g (1lb) sliced*
Plain flour - *25g (1oz)*
Salt *and freshly ground* **black pepper**
Beef stock - *75ml (5 tbsp)*
Fresh milk - *300ml (½ pint)*
Garlic clove - *1, crushed*
Mixed herbs - *large pinch*
Canned tomatoes - *397g (14oz) can, chopped*
Bacon - *4 rashers, for garnish*

METHOD

1 Gently fry the onions in the butter until soft.

2 Coat the liver in seasoned flour, add to the onions and brown on all sides.

3 Gradually stir in the stock, milk, garlic, herbs and tomatoes. Place in an ovenproof casserole and bake at 190°C (375°F), mark 5 for 15-20 minutes.

4 Roll up strips of bacon, thread on a skewer and grill until crisp. Serve hot garnished with bacon rolls.

330 Calories per portion

Kidney Stroganoff

SERVES 4

Butter - *25g (1oz)*
Onion - *1 small, finely chopped*
Button mushrooms - *100g (4oz) sliced*
Salt *and freshly ground* **black pepper**
Plain flour - *25g (1oz)*
Lambs kidneys - *8, skinned, cored and quartered*
Fresh milk - *300ml (½ pint)*
Natural yogurt - *150g (5oz) low fat*
Parsley - *chopped for garnish*

METHOD

1 Melt the butter in a frying pan and gently fry the onion until soft. Add the mushrooms.

2 Season the flour and use to coat the kidneys. Add kidneys and any remaining flour to the frying pan and cook for 5 minutes until brown all over.

3 Gradually stir in the milk, season lightly and bring to the boil, stirring continuously. Cover and simmer for 10 minutes. Remove pan from the heat, stir in most of the yogurt and reheat without boiling. Serve garnished with yogurt and parsley.

515 Calories per portion

Chicken Liver & Mushroom Pie

SERVES 6

Butter - *40g (1½ oz)*
Chicken livers - *450g (1lb)*
Onion - *1 medium, finely chopped*
Button mushrooms - *100g (4oz) sliced*
Fresh milk - *300ml (½ pint)*
Plain flour - *25g (1oz)*
Dried mixed herbs - *2.5ml (½ tsp)*
Salt *and freshly ground* **black pepper**

Canned tomatoes - *400g (14oz) can, drained*
Red pepper - *1 large, blanched, de-seeded and sliced*
Fresh double cream - *30ml (2 tbsp)*
Frozen puff pastry - *375g (13oz) thawed*

METHOD

1 Melt the butter in a frying pan and sauté the livers for 3 minutes. Remove from the pan. Add the onions and mushrooms and cook until soft.

2 Add the milk, flour and herbs and heat, stirring continuously until the sauce thickens and boils. Season lightly and cook for one minute.

3 Add the drained tomatoes, red pepper and livers and simmer for 3 minutes. Stir in the cream and pour into a 1.7 litre (3 pint) pie dish.

4 Roll out the pastry 0.5cm (¼ inch) thick and use to cover the pie dish, decorate with pastry leaves and brush with milk. Bake at 230°C (450°F), mark 8 for 10 minutes then lower the heat and bake at 190°C (375°F), mark 5 for 15-20 minutes or until the pastry is well risen.

385 Calories per portion Ⓕ

Tomato Quiche SERVES 4

Plain flour - *175g (6oz)*
Salt *and freshly ground* black pepper
Butter - *75g (3oz) diced*
Tomatoes - *350g (12oz) sliced*
Onion - *1 small, chopped*
Fresh basil - *5ml (1 tsp) chopped*
Fresh parsley - *5ml (1 tsp) chopped*

Dried thyme - *5ml (1 tsp)*
Egg - *1 (size 3)*
Fresh milk - *200ml (7 fl oz)*
Tomato slices - *for garnish*

METHOD

1 Sift the flour and a pinch of salt in a bowl. Rub in
the butter until mixture resembles fine breadcrumbs.
Add 30-45ml (2-3 tbsp) water and mix to a dough.
Roll out and use to line a 20.5cm (8 inch) flan dish.
Bake 'blind' at 200°C (400°F), mark 6 for 15 minutes.

2 Simmer the tomatoes, onion and herbs in
30ml (2 tbsp) water until soft. Season lightly.

3 Beat the egg and milk together and stir into the
tomatoes. Pour into the pastry case and bake at
180°C (350°F), mark 4 for 35-40 minutes.
Serve hot or cold, garnished with tomato.

465 Calories per portion Ⓕ

Smoked Ham & Leek Flan SERVES 4

Wholemeal flour - *175g (6oz)*
Butter - *75g (3oz)*
Salt *and freshly ground* black pepper
Leek - *1, washed and sliced*
Eggs - *2 (size 3) beaten*
Fresh milk - *300ml (½ pint)*
Smoked ham - *50g (2oz) cubed*
Red Leicester cheese - *50g (2oz) grated*

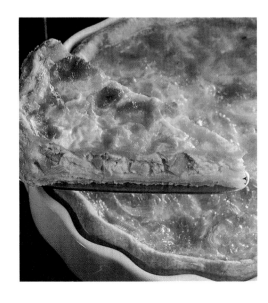

METHOD

1 Sift flour and a pinch of salt in a bowl. Rub in the
butter until mixture resembles fine breadcrumbs.
Add 45-60ml (3-4 tbsp) water and mix to a dough.
Roll out and use to line a 20.5cm (8 inch) flan ring.
Bake 'blind' at 200°C (400°F), mark 6 for
15 minutes.

2 Blanch the leek for 2 minutes. Drain well.

3 Beat the eggs and milk. Add the leek, smoked
ham and cheese. Season with pepper and pour into
the pastry case. Bake at 180°C (350°F), mark 4 for
35-40 minutes or until set. Serve hot or cold.

345 Calories per portion Ⓕ

Onion Tart
SERVES 6

Plain flour - *175g (6oz)*
Butter - *115g (4½ oz)*
Salt *and freshly ground* **black pepper**
Onions - *550g (1¼ lb) sliced*
Eggs - *2 (size 3)*
Fresh milk - *225ml (8 fl oz)*

METHOD

1 Sift the flour and a pinch of salt into a bowl.
Rub in 75g (3 oz) butter until the mixture resembles
fine breadcrumbs. Add 30-45ml (2-3 tbsp)
water and mix to a dough. Roll out and use to line
a 20.5cm (8 inch) flan ring.

2 Melt the remaining butter in a large frying pan.
Add the onions and season lightly. Cook gently,
without browning, until they start to soften.
Place in the flan case.

3 Beat the eggs and milk and pour over the onions.
Bake at 220°C (425°F), mark 7 for 35-40 minutes
until set and golden.

---

445 Calories per portion

Chilled Cheese Flan
SERVES 4

Plain flour - *175g (6oz)*
Butter - *75g (3oz) diced*
Gelatine - *10ml (2 tsp)*
Greek style yogurt - *150g (5oz)*
Fresh milk - *45ml (3 tbsp)*
Made mustard - *5ml (1 tsp)*

Cheshire cheese - *75g (3oz) finely grated*
Cucumber - *5cm (2 inch) piece, peeled and grated*
Salt *and freshly ground* **black pepper**
Egg white* - *1, stiffly whisked*
Cucumber and red pepper - *to garnish*
*see page 2

METHOD

1 Sift the flour and a pinch of salt into a bowl. Rub in
the butter until mixture resembles fine breadcrumbs.
Add 30-40ml (2-3 tbsp) water and mix to a dough.
Roll out and use to line a 20.5cm (8 inch) flan ring.
Bake 'blind' at 200°C (400°F), mark 6 for 15 minutes
then at 180°C (350°F), mark 4 for 15 minutes.

2 Sprinkle the gelatine over 30ml (2 tbsp) hot
water in a basin over a pan of simmering water.
Stir until dissolved. Cool slightly.

3 Mix the yogurt, milk and mustard together. Stir
in the gelatine, cheese and cucumber. Season lightly.

4 Fold 15ml (1 tbsp) whisked egg white into the
cheese mixture with a metal spoon then fold in the
remainder. Pour into the pastry case. Chill until set
and serve garnished with cucumber and red
pepper.

375 Calories per portion

Vegetable Layer

SERVES 4

Potatoes - *450g (1lb), sliced*
Cauliflower - *½ large, broken into florets*
Carrots - *225g (8oz) sliced*
Mushrooms - *50g (2oz) sliced*
Green beans - *100g (4oz) fresh or frozen*
Salt *and freshly ground* **black pepper**

Vegetarian English Cheddar cheese - *100g (4oz) grated*
Eggs - *2 (size 3) beaten*
Fresh milk - *300ml (½ pint)*

METHOD

1 Place layers of potato, cauliflower, carrots, mushrooms, beans and cheese in a buttered casserole dish. Season lightly. Repeat the layers until all vegetables are used up.

2 Beat eggs and milk together, season lightly and pour over the vegetables. Bake, uncovered, at 180°C (350°F), mark 4 for 1½ hours or until set and golden.

340 Calories per portion

Vegetable Curry

SERVES 4

Oil - *15-30ml (1-2 tbsp)*
Onion - *1 medium, chopped*
Curry powder - *15ml (1 tbsp) or to taste*
Paprika pepper - *5ml (1 tsp)*
Tomato purée - *10ml (2 tsp)*
Lemon juice - *5ml (1 tsp)*
Apricot jam or redcurrant jelly - *15ml (1 tbsp)*
Fresh milk - *300ml (½ pint)*
Sultanas - *50g (2oz)*

Raw mixed vegetables -
  cauliflower, carrots, potatoes - 1kg (2.2lb)
Eggs - *4 (size 3) hard boiled*
Watercress - *for garnish*

METHOD

1 Pour oil into a large saucepan and gently fry the onion for a few minutes without browning. Add curry powder and paprika and cook for a further 3 minutes.

2 Add tomato purée, lemon juice, jam, milk and sultanas, bring almost to the boil and simmer, uncovered, for 10 minutes.

3 Cook the vegetables – cut in bite-sized pieces – in boiling salted water for 10 minutes. Drain well, add to the sauce and continue simmering until the vegetables are just tender. Serve garnished with hard-boiled egg and watercress.

Vegetarian

520 Calories per portion

Potato Layer Bake SERVES 4

Potatoes - *1kg (2.2lb) thinly sliced*
Onion - *1 large, thinly sliced*
Butter - *25g (1oz)*
Vegetarian English Cheddar cheese - *175g (6oz) grated*
Salt *and freshly ground* **black pepper**
Fresh milk - *300ml (½ pint)*
Parsley - *for garnish*

METHOD

1 Layer potatoes, onion, knobs of butter and cheese in an ovenproof casserole, finishing with a layer of cheese.

2 Lightly season the milk and pour over the vegetables. Bake at 190°C (375°F), mark 5 for 1½ hours or until the potatoes are cooked and the top golden. Serve garnished with parsley.

---

425 Calories per portion Ⓕ

Golden Vegetable Bake SERVES 4

Potatoes - *450g (1lb) sliced*
Butter - *25g (1oz)*
Raw mixed vegetables - *cauliflower, leek, carrots - 1kg (2.2lb)*
Fresh milk - *300ml (½ pint)*
Vegetable stock or water - *150ml (¼ pint)*
Dried vegetable soup mix - *568ml (1 pint) pkt*
Vegetarian English Cheddar cheese - *100g (4oz) grated*
Salt *and freshly ground* **black pepper**

METHOD

1 Cook potatoes in boiling water for 5 minutes. Drain and put aside.

2 Melt the butter in a large saucepan and fry the vegetables-cut into medium-sized pieces-for a few minutes without browning. Stir in the milk and stock, bring to the boil and simmer until the vegetables are just tender. Drain the vegetables, reserving the liquid, and arrange them in a shallow ovenproof dish.

3 Place the packet soup mix in a saucepan, stir in the reserved liquid and heat stirring continuously until the mixture boils. Remove from the heat, cool slightly, stir in half the cheese and pour over the vegetables.

4 Cover the top with slices of potato, sprinkle with the remaining cheese and bake at 200°C (400°F), mark 6 for 20 minutes or until golden brown.

470 Calories per portion Ⓕ

Parsnip & Tomato Bake SERVES 4

Parsnips - *2 large, peeled and sliced*
Leeks - *2 large, washed and sliced*
Pasta shells - *100g (4oz)*
Fresh milk - *300ml (½ pint)*
Butter - *25g (1oz)*
Plain flour - *25g (1oz)*
Salt *and freshly ground* **black pepper**

Cayenne pepper - *large pinch*
Made mustard - *5ml (1 tsp)*
Vegetarian English Cheddar cheese - *150g (5oz) grated*
Tomatoes - *3, skinned and sliced*
Fresh breadcrumbs - *50g (2oz) grated*

METHOD

1 Cook parsnips and leeks in boiling salted water for 10 minutes until just tender. Drain well.

2 Cook pasta according to the instructions on the packet and mix with the cooked vegetables.

3 Place milk, butter and flour in a saucepan and heat, stirring continuously until the sauce thickens and boils. Season lightly, add the cayenne and mustard and cook for one minute. Remove from the heat and stir in 75g (3oz) cheese.

4 Place half the vegetable mixture in the base of a buttered ovenproof dish, cover with a layer of tomato, then half the sauce. Repeat the layers, finishing with sauce. Mix remaining cheese with the breadcrumbs and sprinkle over the top. Bake at 190°C (375° F), mark 5 for 30 minutes or until golden.

435 Calories per portion Ⓕ

Creamy Courgette Tart SERVES 6

Plain flour - *175g (6oz)*
Pinch of salt
Pinch of cayenne pepper
Butter - *75g (3oz) diced*
Vegetarian English Cheddar cheese - *100g (4oz) grated*
Courgettes - *450g (1lb)*
Eggs - *2 (size 3)*
Fresh double cream - *150ml (5 fl oz)*

METHOD

1 Place flour and seasoning in a bowl. Rub in the butter until mixture resembles fine breadcrumbs and stir in half the cheese. Add 15-30ml (1-2 tbsp) water and mix to a dough. Knead lightly and roll out to line a 20.5cm (8 inch) flan ring. Bake 'blind' at 190°C (375°F), mark 5 for 20 minutes. Cool.

2 Cut the courgettes into 1cm (½ inch) slices and cook in boiling, salted water for 8 minutes. Drain well, dry on kitchen paper and arrange in the pastry case.

3 Beat the eggs and cream, season lightly, add the remaining cheese and pour over the courgettes. Bake at 190°C (375°F), mark 5 for 30 minutes until golden. Serve hot or cold.

425 Calories per portion Ⓕ

Cheshire Aubergine Layer

SERVES 4

Aubergines - *700g (1½ lb) sliced*
Salt *and freshly ground* **black pepper**
Butter - *40g (1½oz)*
Onion - *1 small, chopped*
Garlic clove - *1, chopped*
Tomatoes - *450g (1lb) skinned and chopped*
Plain flour - *25g (1oz)*
Fresh milk - *300ml (½ pint)*
Natural yogurt - *30ml (2 tbsp) low fat*
Vegetarian Cheshire cheese - *100g (4oz) grated*
Olive oil - *45-60ml (3-4 tbsp)*

METHOD

1 Place the aubergines in a colander, sprinkle with salt, cover with a weighted plate and leave to drain for ½ – 1 hour. Dry well on kitchen paper.

2 Melt 15g (½ oz) butter and gently fry the onion and garlic until soft, add the tomatoes and simmer for 5 minutes.

3 Place the flour, milk and remaining butter in a saucepan and heat, stirring continuously until the sauce thickens and boils. Season lightly and cook for one minute. Remove from the heat and stir in the yogurt and 50g (2oz) cheese.

4 Fry the aubergines in hot oil until golden. Drain on kitchen paper.

5 Arrange one third of the aubergines on the base of an ovenproof dish, cover with half the tomatoes then half the sauce. Repeat the layers, finishing with aubergines. Sprinkle with the remaining cheese and bake at 180°C (350°F), mark 4 for 40 minutes. Serve immediately.

305 Calories per portion Ⓕ

Aubergine Tart

SERVES 6

Aubergines - *350g (12oz) sliced*
Salt *and freshly ground* **black pepper**
Plain flour - *175g (6oz)*
Butter - *75g (3oz) diced*
Olive oil - *15-30ml (1-2 tbsp)*

Tomatoes - *4, skinned and chopped*
Dried oregano - *5ml (1 tsp)*
Lemon juice - *30ml (2 tbsp)*
Eggs - *2 (size 3)*
Fresh milk - *150ml (¼ pint)*

METHOD

1 Place aubergines in a colander, sprinkle with salt, cover with a weighted plate and leave to drain for ½-1 hour. Dry well on kitchen paper.

2 Place the flour and a pinch of salt in a bowl. Rub in the butter until the mixture resembles fine breadcrumbs. Add 15-30ml (1-2 tbsp) water and mix to a dough. Knead lightly and roll out to line a 20.5cm (8 inch) flan dish.

3 Fry aubergines in hot oil until golden. Add tomatoes, oregano and lemon juice, season lightly and cook for 5 minutes. Arrange in the pastry case.

4 Mix the eggs and milk, pour into the flan case and bake at 200°C (400°F), mark 6 for 30 minutes.

445 Calories per portion

Spanish Omelette SERVES 4

Green pepper - *75g (3oz) de-seeded and cored*
Butter - *50g (2oz)*
Potatoes - *450g (1lb) peeled and diced*
Onions - *225g (8oz) chopped*
Salt *and freshly ground* **black pepper**

Eggs - *4 (size 2)*
Fresh milk - *60ml (4 tbsp)*
Vegetarian English Cheddar cheese - *100g (4oz)*
Parsley - *chopped for garnish*

METHOD

1 Chop the pepper and blanch in boiling water for 2 minutes. Drain.

2 Melt the butter in a large frying pan, add the potatoes and onions, season lightly and cook slowly, turning occasionally, until almost cooked. Raise the heat, add the pepper and continue to cook until the vegetables are turning brown.

3 Beat the eggs and milk and season lightly. Pour over the vegetables, stirring once or twice to spread the mixture evenly. Cook until the underside is golden.

4 Scatter the cheese over the omelette and place under a pre-heated grill until the cheese is bubbling and golden brown. Serve sprinkled with parsley.

290 Calories per portion

Individual Cheese & Garlic Soufflés SERVES 4

Plain flour - *25g (1oz)*
Butter - *25g (1oz)*
Fresh milk - *150ml (¼ pint)*
Salt *and freshly ground* **black pepper**
Vegetarian English Cheddar cheese - *100g (4oz) finely grated*
Garlic cloves - *2, crushed*
Eggs - *3 (size 2) separated*

METHOD

1 Place the flour, butter and milk into a saucepan, heat, stirring continuously until the sauce thickens and boils. Season lightly and cook for one minute. Remove from the heat and cool slightly.

2 Stir the finely, grated cheese, garlic and egg yolks into the sauce.

3 Whisk the egg whites until stiff and gently fold 15ml (1 tbsp) into the sauce with a metal spoon. Fold in the remaining egg white. Pour into 4 buttered ramekin dishes. Bake at 200°C (400°F), mark 6 for 20 minutes. Serve immediately.

355 Calories per portion Ⓕ

Blue Stilton Flan SERVES 6

Wholemeal flour - *175g (6oz)*
Butter - *90g (3½ oz)*
Salt *and freshly ground* **black pepper**
Tomatoes - *4, skinned and sliced*
Fresh milk - *150ml (¼ pint)*

Plain flour - *15g (½ oz)*
Stilton cheese - *100g (4oz)*
Eggs - *1 (size 3), separated*
Onion - *1 small, sliced*

METHOD

1 Place flour and a pinch of salt in a bowl. Rub in 75g (3oz) butter until the mixture resembles fine breadcrumbs. Add 15-30ml (1-2 tbsp) water and mix to a soft dough. Knead lightly and roll out to line a 20.5cm (8 inch) flan ring.

2 Arrange most of the tomato in the base of the flan ring.

3 Place milk, plain flour and remaining butter in a saucepan and heat, stirring continuously until the sauce thickens and boils. Remove from the heat.

4 Add the egg yolk and crumbled Stilton then fold in the stiffly whisked egg white. Pour into the flan ring and arrange tomato slices and onion rings on top. Bake at 180°C (350°F), mark 5 for 45 minutes. Serve hot or cold.

365 Calories per portion of fondue

Cheddar Cheese Fondue SERVES 6

Garlic clove - *1*
Dry white wine - *300ml (½ pint)*
Lemon juice - *5ml (1 tsp)*
Vegetarian Cheddar cheese - *450g (1lb) grated*
Cornflour - *15ml (1 tbsp)*
Black pepper - *freshly ground*
Ground nutmeg - *large pinch*
Kirsch - *30ml (2 tbsp)*
French stick - *cubed for serving*

METHOD

1 Rub the inside of a fondue pan with a cut garlic clove. Add the wine and heat gently on the hob over a moderate heat.

2 Gradually add the cheese and cornflour mixed together. Heat stirring continuously until the cheese has melted and the mixture is thick and creamy. Stir in the remaining ingredients and transfer the pan to the fondue burner to keep hot. Serve with French bread.

390 Calories per portion

Cheese & Pickle Potatoes

SERVES 6

Baked potatoes - *6 large*
Butter - *15g (½ oz)*
Vegetarian Red Leicester cheese - *175g (6oz) finely grated*
Fresh milk - *45ml (3 tbsp)*
Eggs - *4 (size 3) separated*
Sweet pickle - *15ml (1 tbsp)*
Salt *and freshly ground* **black pepper**

METHOD

1 Prick the potatoes all over and bake at 200°C (400°F), mark 6 for 1½ hours.

2 Cut the potatoes in half, scoop out the flesh and mix this in a bowl with the butter, finely grated cheese, milk, egg yolks and pickle.

3 Whisk the whites until stiff and fold lightly into the potato mixture with a metal spoon. Season lightly and pile back into the potato skins. Return to the oven and bake a further 15 minutes until risen and golden. Serve immediately.

350 Calories per portion

Cheese & Egg Footballs

SERVES 8

Potatoes - *700g (1½ lb)*
Butter - *40g (1½ oz)*
English Cheddar cheese - *100g (4oz) grated*
Fresh milk - *30ml (2 tbsp)*
Salt *and freshly ground* **black pepper**
Eggs - *4 (size 3) hard boiled*
Spring onions - *4, finely chopped*
Egg - *1 (size 3) beaten*
Dried breadcrumbs - *for coating*

METHOD

1 Cook the potatoes. Drain well and mash with the butter, cheese and milk. Season lightly.

2 Coarsely chop the hard boiled eggs. Stir into the potato along with the spring onions.

3 Divide into 8 and roll into 'footballs'. Brush with beaten egg and roll in breadcrumbs. Chill.

4 Fry the 'footballs' in deep fat until crisp and golden. Drain well on kitchen paper. Serve immediately.

370 Calories per portion Ⓕ

Peanut Roast

SERVES 6

Peanuts - *225g (8oz) finely chopped*
Wholemeal breadcrumbs - *150g (5oz)*
Rolled oats - *50g (2oz)*
Onion - *1 large, finely chopped*
Carrot - *1, finely grated*
Dried sage - *2.5ml (½ tsp)*
Yeast extract - *10ml (2 tsp)*
Fresh milk - *200ml (7 fl oz)*
Vegetarian English Cheddar cheese - *25g (1oz)*
Canned chopped tomatoes - *425g (15oz) can*
Garlic clove - *1, crushed*
Dried mixed herbs - *2.5ml (½ tsp)*
Salt *and freshly ground* **black pepper**

METHOD

1 Mix the nuts, breadcrumbs, oats, onion, carrot and sage in a large bowl.

2 Dissolve the yeast extract in 10ml (2 tsp) hot water and stir into the nut mixture. Blend in the milk and transfer into a buttered 900g (2lb) loaf tin. Sprinkle with cheese and bake at 190°C (375°F), mark 5 for 45 minutes.

3 Place tomatoes, garlic and mixed herbs in a saucepan. Season and simmer for 10 minutes. Serve with the nut roast.

---

280 Calories per portion

Cheesy Peanut Scone

SERVES 8

Plain flour - *100g (4oz)*
Baking powder - *15ml (3 tsp)*
Mustard powder - *2.5ml (½ tsp)*
Salt *and freshly ground* **black pepper**
Wholemeal flour - *100g (4oz)*
Butter - *50g (2oz)*
Peanuts - *50g (2oz) finely chopped*
Egg - *1 (size 3) beaten*

Fresh milk - *150ml (¼ pint)*
Crunchy peanut butter - *60ml (4 tbsp)*
Cottage cheese - *225g (8oz)*
Lettuce and tomato - *for garnish*

METHOD

1 Sift the plain flour, baking powder and mustard into a bowl. Season lightly. Stir in the wholemeal flour. Rub in the butter until the mixture resembles fine breadcrumbs. Stir in the peanuts. Beat egg and milk, stir into the flour and mix to a soft dough.

2 Knead lightly on a floured surface and divide in two. Roll each into a 20.5cm (8 inch) circle. Mark one circle into eight. Place on greased baking sheets, brush with milk and bake at 230°C (450°F), mark 8 for 15-20 minutes. Cool.

3 Spread the scone with peanut butter then cover with cottage cheese. Lay lettuce leaves and sliced tomato on top and cover with the marked scone.

275 Calories per portion Ⓕ

Dorset Apple Tart SERVES 6

PASTRY
Plain flour - *100g (4oz)*
Butter - *50g (2oz)*
Egg - *1 (size 3) beaten*

FILLING
Butter - *15g (½ oz)*
Cornflour - *25g (1oz)*
Fresh milk - *300ml (½ pint)*
Caster sugar - *25g (1oz)*
Egg - *1 (size 3) yolk only*
Vanilla essence - *2.5ml (½ tsp)*
Cooking apples - *225g (8oz) peeled and sliced*
Demerara sugar - *25g (1oz)*
Cinnamon - *5ml (1 tsp)*

METHOD

1 Place flour and a pinch of salt in a bowl. Rub in the butter until the mixture resembles fine breadcrumbs. Add sufficient egg to give a soft but not sticky dough. Roll out and use to line a 20.5cm (8 inch) flan ring. Bake blind at 180°C (350°F), mark 4 for 15 minutes.

2 Place butter, cornflour and milk in a saucepan and heat, stirring continuously until the sauce thickens and boils for one minute. Cool slightly. Stir in the sugar, egg yolk and essence. Pour into the flan case.

3 Arrange apple over the sauce and sprinkle with a mixture of demerara and cinnamon.
Bake for a further 20 minutes.

365 Calories per portion

Mincemeat & Apple Tart SERVES 6

Shortcrust pastry - *made with 175g (6oz) flour*
Cooking apple - *1, cored and grated*
Mincemeat - *175g (6oz)*
Fresh double cream - *150ml (5 fl oz)*
Blanched almonds - *25g (1oz) toasted and crushed*

METHOD

1 Roll out pastry and use to line a 20.5cm (8 inch) flan dish.

2 Mix apple and mincemeat and place in the pastry case. Bake at 220°C (400°F), mark 6 for 15 minutes then at 170°C (325°F), mark 3 for 10 minutes. Cool slightly.

3 Lightly whip the cream, spoon over the flan and sprinkle with almonds. Serve immediately.

380 Calories per portion

Date & Lemon Pudding SERVES 6

Plain flour - *75g (3oz)*
Salt - *2.5ml (½ tsp)*
Baking powder - *5ml (1 tsp)*
Sugar - *15g (½ oz)*
Shredded suet - *75g (3oz)*
Fresh white breadcrumbs - *75g (3oz)*
Dates - *75g (3oz) chopped*
Mixed dried fruit - *25g (1oz)*
Lemon - *½, grated rind and juice*
Egg - *1 (size 3) beaten*
Fresh milk - *90ml (6 tbsp)*

SAUCE
Cornflour - *15g (½ oz)*
Custard powder - *15g (½ oz)*
Sugar - *25g (1oz)*
Fresh milk - *450ml (¾ pint)*
Lemon - *1, grated rind and juice*
Butter - *15g (½ oz)*

METHOD

1 Sift flour, salt and baking powder into a large bowl. Stir in remaining ingredients and mix well.

2 Pour into a buttered 900ml (1½ pint) basin, cover with greaseproof paper and foil and secure with string. Steam for 2 hours.

3 Sauce: blend cornflour, custard powder and sugar with 30ml (2 tbsp) milk in a jug. Heat remaining milk until hot. Blend with the cornflour and return to the pan. Heat, stirring continuously, until the mixture thickens and boils. Stir in the lemon rind, juice and butter.

4 Turn pudding out onto a plate and top with sauce.

440 Calories per portion Ⓕ

Christmas Pudding EACH PUDDING SERVES 8

Plain flour - *100g (4oz)*
Mixed spice - *2.5ml (½ tsp)*
Grated nutmeg - *large pinch*
Fresh white breadcrumbs - *225g (8oz)*
Finely shredded suet - *275g (10oz)*
Soft brown sugar - *225g (8oz)*
Seedless raisins - *350g (12oz)*
Sultanas - *350g (12 oz)*
Chopped mixed peel - *50g (2oz)*
Almonds - *50g (2oz) blanched*
Orange - *1, grated rind only*
Eggs - *4 (size 3) beaten*
Fresh milk - *150ml (¼ pint)*
Brandy or dry sherry - *½ wine glass*
Almond essence - *2.5ml (½ tsp)*

METHOD

1 Sift flour, spice and nutmeg into a bowl. Stir in breadcrumbs, suet, sugar, raisins, sultanas, mixed peel, finely chopped almonds and orange rind.

2 Combine with eggs, milk, brandy and almond essence. Mix well and divide between 2 greased and base lined 1 litre (1¾ pint) basins.

3 Cover with greased, pleated, greaseproof paper. Secure with string, using extra string to make a handle.

4 Place a metal trivet in a large saucepan and add boiling water to come halfway up the sides of the basin. Add pudding and cover. Steam for 6 hours, replenishing regularly with boiling water.

5 Remove from the pan and leave to cool. Cover with foil and store in a cool place for at least 2 weeks.

6 To reheat, steam for 2½ hours. Turn out onto a warm plate and serve with brandy sauce or fresh cream.

275 Calories per portion

Butterscotch Apple Meringue

SERVES 6

Cooking apples - *450g (1lb) cored and chopped*
Cornflour - *40g (1½ oz)*
Fresh milk - *450ml (¾ pint)*
Golden syrup - *15ml (1 tbsp)*
Soft brown sugar - *50g (2oz)*
Butter - *15g (½ oz)*
Fresh single cream - *30ml (2 tbsp)*
Eggs - *2 (size 3) whites only*
Caster sugar - *100g (4oz)*

METHOD

1 Cook apples in 30ml (2 tbsp) water until just tender.

2 Blend the cornflour in a jug with a little milk. Heat remaining milk, syrup, sugar and butter until boiling and stir onto the cornflour. Return to the pan and bring to the boil, stirring continuously. Simmer for 3-4 minutes. Cool slightly.

3 Stir in the cream and fold in the apple. Pour into an ovenproof dish.

4 Stiffly whisk the egg whites, whisk in most of the sugar. Fold in the remaining sugar with a metal spoon. Pipe in swirls onto the apple. Bake at 150°C (300°F), mark 2 for 30 minutes until meringue is brown. Serve hot or cold.

265 Calories per portion

Honey Banana Pudding

SERVES 6

Fresh milk - *450ml (¾ pint)*
Butter - *15g (½ oz)*
Lemon - *1, rind only*
Fresh white breadcrumbs - *100g (4oz)*
Eggs - *2 (size 3) separated*
Caster sugar - *100g (4oz)*
Bananas - *2 medium*
Clear honey - *15ml (1 tbsp) warmed*
Demerara sugar - *5ml (1 tsp) to sprinkle*

METHOD

1 Heat milk, butter and lemon rind until the butter has melted. Add breadcrumbs, egg yolks and 25g (1 oz) sugar. Pour into a greased ovenproof dish. Bake at 170°C (325°F), mark 3 for 30 minutes.

2 Slice bananas and mix most of them with the honey. Arrange over the pudding.

3 Stiffly whisk egg whites and fold in the remaining sugar. Pipe onto the pudding and bake at 200°C (400°F), mark 6 for 10 minutes. Decorate with remaining banana, sprinkled with demerara sugar.

310 Calories per portion

Pineapple Pudding SERVES 6

Trifle sponges - *4-6*
Canned pineapple pieces - *425g (15oz) drained*
Butter - *25g (1oz)*
Plain flour - *25g (1oz)*
Fresh milk - *450ml (¾ pint)*
Eggs - *2 (size 3) separated*
Caster sugar - *100g (4oz)*

METHOD

1 Cut sponges in half and place in the base of an ovenproof dish. Soak with pineapple juice and arrange pineapple pieces on top.

2 Place butter, flour and milk in a saucepan, heat stirring until the sauce thickens and boils. Cook for one minute. Cool slightly, beat in the yolks and pour into the dish.

3 Stiffly whisk the egg whites, gradually beat in half the sugar and fold in the remainder. Pipe around the dish and bake at 170°C (325°F), mark 3 for 30 minutes or until brown.

---

355 Calories per portion

Rhubarb Custard Pie SERVES 6

Plain flour - *175g (6oz)*
Pinch of salt
Butter - *75g (3oz) diced*
Caster sugar - *65g (2½ oz)*
Eggs - *2 (size 3) separated*

Rhubarb - *225g (8oz)*
Sugar - *50g (2oz)*
Cornflour - *25g (1oz)*
Fresh milk - *150ml (¼ pint)*

METHOD

1 Place flour and salt in a bowl. Rub in the butter until the mixture resembles fine breadcrumbs. Add 15g (½ oz) caster sugar. Add one yolk and sufficient milk to give a soft dough. Knead lightly and roll out to line a 20.5cm (8 inch) flan ring. Bake 'blind' at 200°C (400°F), mark 6 for 15 minutes.

2 Cook rhubarb and sugar in 30ml (2 tbsp) water until soft.

3 Blend cornflour with a little milk. Add remaining milk to the rhubarb, bring to the boil and stir into blended cornflour. Return to the pan and heat, stirring, until the mixture thickens and boils. Cool slightly, stir in remaining yolk and pour into the case.

4 Stiffly whisk egg whites, fold in remaining caster sugar. Pipe meringue over the flan and bake at 180°C (375°F), mark 4 for 15 minutes. Serve immediately.

460 Calories per portion

Coffee & Walnut Meringue Pie SERVES 6

Digestive biscuits - *225g (8oz) crushed*
Butter - *75g (3oz)*
Cornflour - *40g (1½ oz)*
Coffee granules - *10ml (2 tsp)*
Fresh milk - *450ml (¾ pint)*
Eggs - *2 (size 3) separated*
Plain chocolate - *25g (1oz) grated*
Demerara sugar - *15g (½ oz)*
Chopped walnuts - *25g (1oz)*

Caster sugar - *25g (1oz)*
Coffee essence - *2.5-5ml (½-1 tsp)*

METHOD

1 Mix digestives with melted butter and press into the base and sides of a 20.5cm (8 inch) pie dish. Chill.

2 Blend cornflour, coffee, milk and egg yolks. Heat, stirring continuously until the sauce thickens and boils. Cook for one minute. Remove from the heat and add chocolate, demerara sugar and walnuts. Cool and pour onto biscuit base.

3 Stiffly whisk egg whites. Fold in caster sugar and coffee essence. Pile on top of the mixture and brown under a hot grill.

---

345 Calories per portion

Hot Swiss Trifle SERVES 6

Jam filled swiss roll - *1, sliced*
Canned apricots - *350g (12oz) can, drained*
Custard powder - *30ml (2 tbsp)*
Eggs - *2 (size 3) separated*
Sugar - *15ml (1 tbsp)*
Fresh milk - *568ml (1 pint)*
Caster sugar - *100g (4oz)*
Blanched almonds - *25g (1oz)*

METHOD

1 Arrange swiss roll in the base and around the sides of a 1 litre (1¾ pint) ovenproof dish. Cover with apricots.

2 Blend custard powder, egg yolks and sugar with a little milk in a jug.

3 Heat remaining milk to almost boiling and pour onto custard powder. Return to the pan and heat, stirring until the custard thickens and boils. Cool slightly and pour over the apricots.

2 Stiffly whisk the egg whites, fold in caster sugar and pile on top of the custard. Stud with almonds. Bake at 180°C (350°F), mark 4 for 20 minutes.

405 Calories per portion

Caramelled Fruit Cobbler SERVES 6

Butter - *50g (2oz)*
Self raising flour - *175g (6oz)*
Fresh milk - *150ml (¼ pint)*
Cooking apples - *2 large, cored and sliced*
Canned raspberries - *385g (13½ oz) drained*
Fresh double cream - *150ml (5 fl oz) lightly whipped*
Demerara sugar - *30ml (2 tbsp)*
Raspberry jam - *30ml (2 tbsp) for filling scones*

METHOD

1 Rub butter into flour until mixture
resembles fine breadcrumbs. Add milk and
mix to a soft dough. Knead lightly, roll out and
cut into 14 hearts. Bake at 230°C (450°F),
mark 8 for 7-10 minutes.

2 Cook apples in 30ml (2 tbsp) water until
soft, drain and add raspberries. Place in a
heatproof serving dish.

3 Spread cream over the fruit and sprinkle with
sugar. Grill under a medium heat until sugar
caramelises. Arrange scones – split and sandwich
together with jam – around the edge.
Serve immediately.

340 Calories per portion **F**

Double Crust Apple Pie SERVES 6

Bramley cooking apples - *450g-550g (1-1½ lb)*
                           cored and sliced
Sugar - *25-40g (1-1½ oz)*
Shortcrust pastry - *made using 225g (8oz) flour*

METHOD

1 Cook apples and sugar in 30ml (2 tbsp) water in a
covered saucepan for 10 minutes.

2 Roll out a little more than half the pastry and use
to line a 20.5cm (8 inch) pie plate. Fill with cooked
apple.

3 Moisten edges of pastry with water. Cover with
a lid, rolled and shaped from remaining pastry.
Press edges well together to seal. Flake edges by
cutting lightly with the back of a knife then ridge
with a fork.

4 Brush with milk, make a hole in the centre and
stand pie on a baking sheet. Bake at 200°C (400°F),
mark 6 for 30 minutes. Serve with fresh cream,
yogurt or custard.

500 Calories per portion

Chocolate & Banana Pancakes SERVES 6

Plain flour - *100g (4oz)*
Egg - *1 (size 3)*
Fresh milk - *300ml (½ pint)*
Oil - *for frying pancakes*

Plain chocolate - *100g (4oz) broken in small pieces*
Icing sugar - *50g (2oz)*
Butter - *25g (1oz)*
Bananas - *4 small, sliced*
Banana or hazelnut yogurt - *150g (5oz) carton*
Whipping cream - *150ml (5 fl oz) lightly whipped*
Flaked almonds - *25g (1oz) toasted*

METHOD

1 Sift flour and a pinch of salt into a bowl. Break in the egg.

2 Gradually add half the milk, beating to form a smooth batter. Pour in remaining milk and beat until smooth.

3 Lightly brush a 20.5cm (8 inch) frying pan with oil and when hot, pour in 45ml (3 tbsp) batter, tilting to cover the base.

4 Cook until the pancake moves freely, toss and cook until golden. Make 8 pancakes. Keep warm-between two plates over a pan of hot water.

5 Place chocolate, icing sugar, butter and 15ml (1 tbsp) water in a saucepan. Heat, stirring continuously, until chocolate melts.

6 Mix bananas, yogurt and whipped cream. Layer pancakes with banana mixture, finishing with a pancake. Serve coated with chocolate sauce and flaked almonds.

---

315 Calories per portion using fromage frais / 440 Calories per portion using cream cheese.

St. Clement's Layer SERVES 6

Almond essence - *5ml (1 tsp)*
Pancake batter - *made using 300ml (½ pint) milk*
Cream cheese or fromage frais - *225g (8oz)*
Cottage cheese - *100g (4oz) sieved*
Flaked almonds - *50g (2oz) toasted*
Vanilla essence - *2.5ml (½ tsp)*

Clear honey - *30ml (2 tbsp)*
Lemon juice - *30ml (2 tbsp)*
Oranges - *2 large, peeled and sliced*

METHOD

1 Stir almond essence into the batter. Use to make eight 20.5cm (8 inch) pancakes.

2 Blend cream and cottage cheeses, almonds and vanilla essence.

3 Warm honey and lemon juice in a pan and mix well.

4 Brush each pancake lightly with honey mixture. Place one pancake on an ovenproof plate. Spread with a little cheese mixture. Repeat layers until 4 pancakes have been used. Cover with a layer of sliced orange. Finishing with a pancake, continue until all pancakes and filling have been used.

5 Cover with foil and bake at 180°C (350°F), mark 4 for 20 minutes. Serve decorated with remaining orange slices.

200 Calories per portion

Orange & Rum Butter Pancakes MAKES 12

Butter - *75g (3oz)*
Brown sugar - *75g (3oz)*
Dark rum - *15ml (1 tbsp)*
Orange - *1, grated rind only*
Plain flour - *225g (8oz)*

Pinch of salt
Eggs - *2 (size 3)*
Fresh milk - *450ml (¾ pint)*
Fresh orange juice - *150ml (¼ pint)*
Orange slices and demerara - *to decorate*

METHOD

1 Melt the butter and beat in the sugar, rum and orange rind. Chill.

2 Sift the flour and salt into a bowl. Break in the eggs.

3 Gradually add half the milk and beat until smooth. Pour in the remaining milk and orange juice and beat until smooth.

4 Use batter to make 12 x 20.5cm (8 inch) pancakes.

5 Divide the chilled rum butter between the hot pancakes. Decorate with slices of orange and sprinkle with demerara.

345 Calories per portion

Boozy Bread & Butter Pudding SERVES 6

Sultanas - *50g (2oz)*
Sherry - *1 sherry glass*
Butter - *50g (2oz)*
White bread or currant loaf - *6 medium slices*
Canned apricots - *425g (15oz) can*
Eggs - *3 (size 3)*
Fresh milk - *568ml (1 pint)*

METHOD

1 Soak the sultanas in sherry for 15 minutes.

2 Butter the bread. Place 3 slices in the base and up the sides of a 1½ litre (2½ pint) ovenproof dish.

3 Strain the juice from the fruit and sprinkle half over the bread. Arrange fruit on top.

4 Strain the sultanas, reserving the juice.

5 Sprinkle the sultanas over the fruit then cover with the remaining bread – butter side up – cut into triangles.

6 Beat eggs, milk and sherry, pour over the pudding and stand for 30 minutes.

7 Stand dish in a roasting tin filled 2.5cm (1 inch) deep with water. Bake at 190°C (375°F), mark 5 for 1 hour or until crisp and golden.

305 Calories per portion

Quick Ginger Gateau SERVES 6

Jamaica ginger cake - *1*
Canned mandarin oranges - *325g (11 oz) can, juice and fruit*
Fresh double cream - *150ml (5 fl oz)*
Orange - *1, grated rind only*

METHOD

1 Slice the cake in half lengthwise. Place one half on a serving plate.

2 Moisten both halves of cake with a little mandarin juice.

3 Place the cream and orange rind in a bowl with 15ml (1 tbsp) mandarin juice. Whip until softly stiff and place half in a piping bag.

4 Reserve about one third of mandarins to decorate the gateau, chop the rest. Add chopped mandarins to the remaining cream and use to sandwich the cake together.

5 Pipe cream down the sides of the gateau and decorate with mandarins. Chill before serving.

240 Calories per portion

Pyjama Jelly SERVES 4

Pineapple jelly - *135g (4¾ oz) packet*
Blackcurrant jelly - *135g (4¾ oz) packet*
Fresh milk - *300ml (½ pint)*

METHOD

1 Break the jellies into separate bowls. Pour 300ml (½ pint) boiling water onto each. Stir until completely dissolved and leave to cool at room temperature.

2 When cool, gradually whisk 150ml (¼ pint) milk into each bowl.

3 Pour an equal amount of pineapple jelly into each of 4 individual glasses and place in the refrigerator to set (approx 1 hour).

4 When set, pour a layer of blackcurrant jelly into each glass and refrigerate until set. Continue layering until all the jelly has been used.

N.B. You can make as many stripes as you like by varying the depth of the layers!

210 Calories per portion

Rosy Caramel Fruits SERVES 6

Fresh raspberries - *225g (8oz)*
Fresh blackcurrants - *225g (8oz) topped and tailed*
Fresh blackberries - *225g (8oz)*
Custard - *made with 300ml (½ pint) milk*
Fresh double cream - *150ml (5 fl oz) whipped*
Dark brown sugar - *30ml (6 tsp)*

METHOD

1 Place a mixture of fruits in each of 6 ovenproof ramekin dishes.

2 Cover with cold custard and top with whipped cream. Sprinkle with sugar. Grill until the sugar has caramelised and the top is bubbling and golden brown. Leave to cool, then chill before serving.

455 Calories per portion

Banana Split SERVES 4

Plain chocolate - *75g (3oz)*
Light soft brown sugar - *25g (1oz)*
Bananas - *4 medium*
Dairy ice cream - *300ml (½ pint)*
Fresh whipping cream - *150ml (5 fl oz) whipped*
Glacé cherries and walnuts - *to decorate*

METHOD

1 Gently heat chocolate, sugar and 5 tbsp water in a saucepan until melted. Add 5 tbsp water, bring to the boil, simmer for 25 minutes until thick.

2 Slice bananas lengthwise. Assemble the 'Split' as shown. Serve sauce separately.

245 Calories per portion

Flamboyant Peach SERVES 6

Sherry - *30ml (2 tbsp)*
Sponge flan case - *23cm (9 inch)*
Eggs - *1 (size 3) + 1 (size 3) yolk only*
Fresh milk - *300ml (½ pint)*
Plain flour - *20g (¾ oz)*
Cornflour - *7g (½ tbsp)*
Caster sugar - *50g (2oz)*
Vanilla essence - *few drops*

Canned sliced peaches -
400g (14oz) can, drained
Chopped nuts -
15ml (1 tbsp) toasted

METHOD

1 Sprinkle sherry over the base of the flan.

2 Mix the egg, egg yolk and 30ml (2 tbsp) milk with the flours and sugar in a jug to form a paste. Heat remaining milk and stir into the egg mixture. Return to the pan and heat, stirring, until the sauce boils and thickens. Cook for one minute, stir in vanilla essence. Cool.

3 Spread sauce over the base of the flan, decorate with peaches and sprinkle with nuts.

---

165 Calories per portion

Tangy Lemon Mousse SERVES 4

Lemon jelly - *half a 135g (4¾ oz) packet*
Lemon or orange yogurt - *150g (5oz)*
Natural yogurt - *150g (5oz) low fat*
Fresh milk - *300ml (½ pint)*
Glacé cherries and angelica - *to decorate*

METHOD

1 Split jelly into cubes, put into a basin, add 60ml (4 tbsp) water and place over a pan of simmering water. Heat, stirring occasionally until the jelly has dissolved. Allow to cool without setting.

2 Whisk yogurts and milk into the jelly until frothy. Pour into individual glasses and leave to set. Serve chilled, decorated with glacé cherries and angelica leaves.

280 Calories per portion

Brazilian Bananas SERVES 4

Bananas - *4 medium*
Instant coffee - *5ml (1 tsp)*
Brown sugar - *5ml (1 tsp)*
Fresh double cream - *150ml (5 fl oz)*
Natural yogurt - *150g (5oz) low fat*
Brown sugar - *20ml (4 tsp) to serve*

METHOD

1 Peel bananas and thickly slice into serving dishes.

2 Dissolve the coffee in 5ml (1 tsp) hot water, add sugar and leave to cool.

3 Whip the cream until stiff. Fold in the yogurt and coffee. Pour over the bananas, sprinkle with sugar and chill for several hours before serving.

---

290 Calories per portion

Orange Charlotte SERVES 6

Gelatine - *11g sachet*
Orange - *1, grated rind and juice*
Eggs* - *2 (size 3) separated*
Caster sugar - *50g (2oz)*
Fresh milk - *300ml (½ pint)*

Sponge finger biscuits - *16*
Fresh milk - *to dip sponge fingers in*
Orange yogurt - *150g (5oz)*
Fresh whipping cream - *150ml (5 fl oz)*
Jellied orange and lemon slices - *to decorate*
*See page 2

METHOD

1 Sprinkle the gelatine over the orange juice. Leave to soak.

2 Beat egg yolks and sugar in a bowl. Heat milk with the orange rind to almost boiling. Stir into the yolks. Place the bowl over a pan of simmering water and cook, stirring occasionally, until the custard thickens sufficiently to coat the back of a wooden spoon.

3 Add gelatine to the custard, stirring until melted. Cool.

4 Line the base and sides of a 15cm (6 inch) loose based cake tin with greaseproof paper. Dip the sponge fingers quickly in milk and arrange around the sides of the tin.

5 When the custard is on the point of setting, fold in the yogurt. Stiffly whisk the egg whites and fold in gently with a metal spoon. Pour into the tin. Chill for 3 hours until set.

6 Trim the sponge fingers level with the filling. Run a knife between the dish and fingers then invert over a serving plate. Remove tin, base and greaseproof. Decorate with whipped cream and jellied fruit.

Cold Desserts

390 Calories per portion

Apricot & Almond Flan SERVES 6

Shortcrust pastry - *made with 175g (6oz) flour*
Apricot jam - *60ml (4 tbsp)*
Macaroons or ratafias - *1 cupful, crumbled*
Eggs - *3 (size 3)*
Caster sugar - *15ml (1 tbsp)*
Fresh milk - *300ml (½ pint)*
Almond essence - *2-3 drops*
Canned apricots - *450g (1lb) can, drained*
Blanched almonds - *25g (1oz) toasted*
Juice from apricots - *30ml (2 tbsp)*

METHOD

1 Roll out pastry to line a 20.5cm (8 inch) flan ring.

2 Spread half the jam over the base and sprinkle with macaroons.

3 Beat eggs, sugar, milk and almond essence. Strain the custard into the flan. Bake at 200°C (400°F), mark 6 for 10 minutes then at 180°C (350°F), mark 4 for 30 minutes or until the custard is set. Cool.

4 Arrange well drained apricots over the cold custard and sprinkle with almonds. Melt remaining jam with the apricot juice and brush over the apricots to glaze. Serve chilled.

---

320 Calories per portion

Royal Rice Ring SERVES 6

Pudding rice - *50g (2oz)*
Fresh milk - *750ml (1¼ pint)*
Egg yolk - *1 (size 3)*
Caster sugar - *50g (2oz)*
Cornflour - *25g (1oz)*
Vanilla essence - *few drops*

Gelatine - *half a 11g sachet*
Kirsch - *15ml (1 tbsp)*
Fresh whipping cream - *150ml (5 fl oz) lightly whipped*
Canned apricot halves - *411g (14½ oz) can*
Glacé cherries and angelica - *to decorate*

METHOD

1 Simmer rice in 450ml (¾ pint) milk for 30 minutes or until tender.

2 Blend egg yolk, caster sugar, cornflour and vanilla essence. Warm remaining milk and pour onto egg mixture. Return to the saucepan and heat, stirring continuously until the sauce thickens and boils.

3 Sprinkle gelatine over 30ml (2 tbsp) hot water in a cup. Leave to soak. Stand in a pan of simmering water and stir until gelatine dissolves. Add to custard, along with the kirsch.

4 Stir custard into the rice, followed by half the cream. Turn into a wetted 750ml (1¼ pint) ring mould. Chill. Turn out, fill with apricots and decorate with remaining whipped cream, cherries and angelica.

300 Calories per portion

Upside Down Pineapple Cheesecake SERVES 6

Fresh milk - *450ml (¾ pint)*
Vanilla blancmange powder - *1 sachet*
Trifle sponges - *1 packet*
Canned crushed pineapple - *411g (14½ oz) can, drained*
Cottage cheese - *225g (8oz) sieved*

Lemon - *1, grated rind and juice*
Fresh double cream - *75ml (2½ fl oz)*
Pineapple slices - *4, to decorate*
Glacé cherries and angelica - *to decorate*

METHOD

1 Using the milk, make up the blancmange according to directions on the packet. Cool.

2 Base line a 15cm (6 inch) loose bottomed cake tin with greaseproof paper. Halve the sponges horizontally. Arrange over the base and sides of the tin and moisten with pineapple juice.

3 Blend cottage cheese, lemon rind and juice, 30ml (2 tbsp) cream and crushed pineapple, finely chopped. Whisk in the blancmange and pour into the tin. Chill until set.

4 Trim the sponges level with the mixture. Turn out onto a serving plate. Whip remaining cream and pipe onto the cake. Decorate with pineapple slices, cherries and angelica.

---

510 Calories per portion

Crunchy Sunshine Layer SERVES 4

Butter - *40g (1½ oz)*
Ginger biscuits - *75g (3oz) crushed*
Cornflakes - *50g (2oz) crushed*
Walnut pieces - *25g (1oz) finely chopped*
Custard powder - *30ml (2 tbsp)*
Fresh milk - *568ml (1 pint)*
Caster sugar - *15ml (1 tbsp)*
Ginger preserve - *15ml (1 tbsp)*
Canned pineapple pieces - *350g (12oz) can, drained*
Fresh whipping cream - *75ml (2½ fl oz) whipped*

METHOD

1 Melt butter. Stir in the crushed biscuits, cornflakes and nuts. Cool.

2 Using the custard powder, milk and sugar, make the custard as directed on the packet. Cool. Stir in the ginger preserve and most of the pineapple, finely chopped.

3 Layer the mixture in 4 individual glasses, finishing with the crunchy mixture. Decorate with cream and pineapple pieces.

405 Calories per portion

Rhubarb Ginger Creams

SERVES 4

Rhubarb - *450g (1lb)*
Sugar - *65g (2½ oz)*
Fresh double cream - *150ml (5 fl oz)*
Raspberry yogurt - *75g (2½ oz)*
Ginger biscuits - *100g (4oz) crushed*

METHOD

1 Cook rhubarb in a little water until soft.
Sweeten to taste and purée in a liquidiser.

2 Whip cream until it stands in peaks. Place 30ml (2 tbsp)
in a piping bag. Mix remainder with the yogurt and rhubarb purée.
Chill.

3 Layer rhubarb and biscuits in 4 individual glasses.
Top with whipped cream and biscuit crumbs.
Serve immediately.

195 Calories per portion

Grape & Vanilla Pots

SERVES 4

Fresh milk - *150ml (¼ pint)*
Fresh soured cream - *150ml (5 fl oz)*
Vanilla instant dessert - *65g (2.5 oz) packet*
Lemon - *½, grated rind and juice*
Egg white* - *1 (size 3)*
Grapes - *75g (3 oz)*
Caster sugar - *for 'frosting' grapes*
*See page 2

METHOD

1 Blend milk into the soured cream. Use to
make up the dessert mix as directed on the
packet. Add the lemon juice and rind. Spoon
into 4 individual dishes and chill.

2 Whisk egg white until frothy and dip clusters
of grapes, first in the egg white, then in the
sugar. Place on greaseproof paper and leave
to dry for 2 hours. Serve vanilla pots decorated
with frosted grapes.

340 Calories per portion

Osborne Pudding

SERVES 4

Wholemeal bread - *2 thin slices, crust removed*
Marmalade - *25g (1oz)*
Eggs yolks - *4 (size 3)*
Caster sugar - *40g (1½ oz)*
Fresh milk - *225ml (8 fl oz)*
Sherry or brandy - *10ml (2 tsp)*
Fresh whipping cream - *150ml (5 fl oz)*
Orange slices - *to decorate*

METHOD

1 Spread the bread with marmalade and cut into tiny strips.

2 Beat yolks and sugar together, heat milk to almost boiling and blend with the yolks. Return to the saucepan and heat *gently,* stirring continuously, until the mixture coats the back of a wooden spoon. DO NOT BOIL.

3 Cool custard slightly, then stir in the bread and sherry.

4 Whip cream until softly stiff and fold all but 45ml (3 tbsp) into the custard. Spoon into individual dishes and chill. Serve decorated with remaining cream and orange slices.

---

95 Calories per portion

Melon Surprise

SERVES 4

Melon - *1 medium sized*
Lemon - *1, grated rind and juice*
Gelatine - *half a 11g sachet*
Ground ginger - *2.5-5ml (½-1 tsp)*
Clear honey - *15ml (1 tbsp)*
Natural yogurt - *300g (10oz) low fat*

METHOD

1 Cut the melon in half, discard seeds and remove flesh with a melon baller. Scoop out remaining flesh with a spoon.

2 Purée melon flesh in a blender, add lemon juice and rind and, if necessary, make up to 150ml (¼ pint) with water.

3 Sprinkle gelatine onto 30ml (2 tbsp) hot water in a cup. Stand cup in a pan of simmering water and stir until gelatine dissolves. Add to the melon purée, along with the ginger and honey.

4 Fold in the yogurt and all but 12 melon balls. Spoon into individual dishes. Chill. Serve decorated with melon balls and a sprinkling of ginger.

TIP: Greek style, rather than low fat yogurt, will give a creamier dessert.

500 Calories per portion

Chocolate Lime Flan SERVES 6

Plain chocolate - *65g (2½ oz)*
Butter - *15g (½ oz)*
Digestive biscuits - *175g (6oz) crushed*
White marshmallows - *350g (12oz)*
Fresh milk - *150ml (¼ pint)*
Lime - *1, grated rind and juice*
Fresh whipping cream - *150ml (5 fl oz)*
Grated chocolate and slices of lime - *to decorate*

METHOD

1 Melt chocolate and butter in a saucepan, stir in digestives. Press into the base and sides of a 23cm (9 inch) flan ring.

2 Melt marshmallows and milk in a basin over a pan of hot water. Stir in rind and juice of the lime. Cool.

3 Lightly whip the cream and fold half into the marshmallow mixture. Pour into the flan ring. Chill. Serve decorated with the remaining cream, lime slices and grated chocolate.

275 Calories per portion Ⓕ

Blackberry & Apple Fool SERVES 4

Blackberries - *225g (8oz)*
Bramley apples - *450g (1lb) peeled, cored and sliced*
Sugar - *25-50g (1-2oz)*
Fresh whipping cream - *200ml (7 fl oz)*

METHOD

1 Set aside 4 blackberries for decoration. Cook the remainder with the apple and sugar in 30ml (2 tbsp) water for 10 minutes or until soft. Cool and sieve into a large bowl.

2 Whip the cream until it holds its shape on the whisk. Place 45ml (3 tbsp) in a piping bag and fold the remainder into the fruit.

3 Spoon into individual glasses. Chill. Serve decorated with a swirl of cream and a blackberry.

200 Calories per portion Ⓕ

Gooseberry & Hazelnut Fool

SERVES 4

Gooseberries - *450g (1lb) topped and tailed*
Sugar - *65g (2½ oz)*
Custard powder - *15ml (1 tbsp)*
Fresh milk - *300ml (½ pint)*
Hazelnut yogurt - *150g (5oz)*
Chopped hazelnuts - *toasted, to decorate*

METHOD

1 Cook gooseberries with 50g (2oz) sugar in a little water until soft. Sieve the fruit or purée in a blender.

2 Blend the remaining sugar and custard powder with 30ml (2 tbsp) milk. Bring remaining milk to the boil. Pour onto custard powder, while stirring and return to the pan. Bring to the boil, stirring continuously. Cool.

3 Combine the custard, gooseberry purée and yogurt then pour into individual glasses. Serve chilled, decorated with toasted hazelnuts.

365 Calories per portion

Lemon Cream Tart

SERVES 6

Gingernut biscuits - *50g (2oz) crushed*
Digestive biscuits - *50g (2oz) crushed*
Butter - *50g (2oz)*
Gelatine - *half a 11g sachet*
Eggs* - *2 (size 3) separated*
Lemon - *1, finely grated rind and juice*
Caster sugar - *100g (4oz)*

Fresh milk - *150ml (¼ pint)*
Fresh whipping cream -
   150ml (5 fl oz) lightly whipped
Lemon slices - *to decorate*
*See page 2.

METHOD

1 Mix crushed biscuits with melted butter. Press into the base of 23cm (9 inch) flan dish.

2 Sprinkle gelatine over 30ml (2 tbsp) hot water in a bowl over a pan of hot water. Stir until dissolved.

3 Whisk egg yolks, lemon rind and juice and half the sugar in a bowl. Stir in the gelatine, milk and half the cream.

4 Whisk the egg whites until stiff and fold in the remaining sugar. Gently fold into the lemon mixture.

5 Pour onto the biscuit base. Chill. Serve decorated with remaining cream and lemon slices.

300 Calories per portion Ⓕ

Gooseberry & Mango Whip SERVES 4

Gelatine - *11g sachet*
Fresh milk - *300ml (½ pint)*
Gooseberries - *225g (8oz) topped and tailed*
Sugar - *40g (1½ oz)*
Lemon - *1, grated rind only*
Canned mangoes - *425g (15oz) can, drained*
Fresh whipping cream - *150ml (5 fl oz) lightly whipped*
Egg white* - *1 (size 3)*
Langues de chat biscuits - *to serve*
*See page 2

METHOD

1 Sprinkle gelatine over 30ml (2 tbsp) hot water in a basin. Stand over a pan of hot water, stirring until dissolved. Stir into the milk. Cool slightly.

2 Cook gooseberries and sugar in 30ml (2 tbsp) water for 10-15 minutes until tender. Add the lemon rind. Cool.

3 Reserve a little mango for decoration and sieve or liquidise the remainder with the gooseberries.

4 Fold the fruit purée, whipped cream and stiffly whisked egg white into the milk as it begins to thicken. Pour into individual glasses. Chill. Serve decorated with chopped mango and langues de chat.

---

450 Calories per portion

Cherry & Almond Flan SERVES 6

Plain flour - *175g (6oz)*
Pinch of salt
Butter - *75g (3oz) cubed*
Cornflour - *25g (1oz)*
Egg* - *1 (size 3) separated*
Caster sugar - *25g (1 oz)*

Almond essence - *2.5ml (½ tsp)*
Fresh milk - *300ml (½ pint)*
Black cherry pie filling - *425g (15oz) can*
Fresh whipping cream - *150ml (5 fl oz) lightly whipped*
Toasted almonds - *to decorate*
*See page 2

METHOD

1 Place flour and salt in a bowl. Rub in the butter until the mixture resembles fine breadcrumbs. Add sufficient water to mix to a soft dough. Knead lightly and roll out to line a 20.5cm (8 inch) flan ring. Bake 'blind' at 190°C (375°F), mark 5 for 15 minutes. Cool.

2 Blend cornflour, egg yolk, sugar and essence with a little milk. Boil the remaining milk, pour onto the cornflour, while stirring, and return to the pan. Heat, stirring continuously until the custard thickens and boils. Cool.

3 Whisk the egg white until stiff. Fold into the custard. Pour into the pastry case and chill.

4 Arrange pie filling over the custard. Serve chilled, decorated with whipped cream and toasted almonds.

530 Calories per portion

Fruit Brulée Tartlets SERVES 4

Plain flour - *100g (4oz)*
Pinch of salt
Caster sugar - *5ml (1 tsp)*
Butter - *75g (3oz) diced*
Egg - *1 (size 3) beaten*
Satsumas - *3, segmented*

Black grapes - *100g (4oz) halved and seeded*
Fresh double cream - *150ml (5 fl oz)*
Caster sugar - *40g (1½ oz)*

METHOD

1 Place flour, salt and sugar in a bowl. Rub in the butter until the mixture resembles fine breadcrumbs. Add the egg, stirring with a round bladed knife until the mixture starts to bind. Collect the mixture together, knead lightly and leave in a cool place for 30 minutes.

2 Roll out and use to line four 10cm (4 inch) tartlet tins. Bake 'blind' at 190°C (375°F), mark 6 for 10 minutes. Cool then remove from the tins.

3 Arrange satsumas and grapes in the tartlets. Whip the cream until softly stiff and spread over the fruit. Smooth the surface and sprinkle each tartlet with sugar. Place under a pre-heated grill for 2-3 minutes until the sugar has caramelised. Chill well before serving.

285 Calories per portion Ⓕ

Wensleydale Apple Cream SERVES 4

Bramley apples - *450g (1lb) cored and sliced*
Lemon - *1, juice only*
Custard powder - *15g (½ oz)*
Fresh milk - *150ml (¼ pint)*
Clear honey - *15ml (1 tbsp) warmed*
Sultanas - *25g (1oz)*
Wensleydale cheese - *100g (4oz) finely grated*
Fresh whipping cream - *75ml (2½ fl oz)*
Toasted almonds and apple slices - *to decorate*

METHOD

1 Cook the apples in the lemon juice over a low heat until tender.

2 Blend custard powder with 30ml (2 tbsp) milk. Bring remaining milk to the boil. Pour onto custard powder, while stirring, and return to the pan. Bring to the boil, stirring continuously. Stir in the apple and allow to cool.

3 Stir honey, sultanas and cheese into the custard and fold in the cream – lightly whipped. Spoon into individual dishes. Chill and serve decorated with apple slices and nuts.

Cold Desserts

180 Calories per portion

Raspberry Cream Meringues SERVES 6

Egg whites - *2 (size 3)*
Caster sugar - *100g (4oz)*
Fresh or frozen raspberries - *225g (8oz)*
Fresh whipping cream -
150ml (5 fl oz) whipped

METHOD

1 Cover a baking sheet with a sheet of non-stick paper.

2 Whisk whites until stiff. Gradually add 50g (2oz) sugar, whisking until the meringue is shiny and stands in peaks. Fold in remaining sugar with a metal spoon. Spoon into a piping bag fitted with a large star nozzle and pipe 12 rounds onto the baking sheet.

3 Bake at 110°C (225°F), mark ¼ for 1½ hours. Carefully peel meringues away from the paper, press a small hole in the underside and stand them upside down on the baking sheet. Return to the oven for ¾ hour. Cool.

4 Fold raspberries into the cream and use to sandwich the meringues together. Serve immediately.

385 Calories per portion

Strawberry Almond Meringues SERVES 4

Icing sugar - *100g (4oz)*
Egg whites - *2 (size 3)*
Ground almonds - *50g (2oz)*
Fresh whipping cream - *150ml (5 fl oz) lightly whipped*
Fresh strawberries - *225g (8oz)*
Flaked almonds - *15g (½ oz), toasted*

METHOD

1 Line a baking sheet with non-stick paper.

2 Lightly whisk the egg whites in a heatproof bowl. Place over a pan of simmering water. Sift icing sugar onto the whites and whisk together until the meringue is thick and holds its shape. Fold in the ground almonds.

3 Place in a piping bag fitted with a fluted nozzle and pipe four rounds onto the baking sheet. Bake at 130°C (250°F), mark ½ for 2 hours, until crisp. Peel off paper and cool.

4 Serve meringues topped with whipped cream, strawberries and toasted almonds.

230 Calories per portion

Kiwi Custard Nests SERVES 6

Custard powder - *15ml (1 tbsp)*
Sugar - *15g (½ oz)*
Fresh milk - *150ml (¼ pint)*
Fresh double cream - *150ml (5 fl oz)*
Meringue nests - *1 packet of 6*
Kiwi fruit - *1, peeled and sliced*
Fresh strawberries - *6, halved*
Peach - *1, peeled and sliced*
Grapes - *6, halved*

METHOD

1 Blend custard powder and sugar with 45ml (3 tbsp) milk. Bring remaining milk and cream to the boil. Pour onto the custard powder, while stirring, and return to the pan. Bring to the boil, stirring continuously. Cool.

2 Spoon custard into the meringue nests and serve chilled, topped with fresh fruit.

370 Calories per portion with fresh fruit

Fruit & Cream Meringues SERVES 3

Egg whites - *2 (size 3)*
Caster sugar - *100g (4oz)*
Fresh whipping cream - *150ml (5 fl oz), lightly whipped*
Fresh fruit - *350g (12oz) raspberries, mandarins*
OR
Canned fruit - *425g (15oz) can, drained*

METHOD

1 Draw three 7cm (3 inch) circles on a piece of non-stick paper and place, pencil mark side down, on a baking sheet.

2 Whisk whites until stiff. Gradually add 50g (2oz) sugar, whisking until the meringue is shiny and stands in peaks. Fold in remaining sugar with a metal spoon. Cover the circles with the mixture.

3 Bake at 140°C (275°F), mark 1 for 35-45 minutes, until golden and crisp – the insides should be fairly soft.

4 Place 45ml (3 tbsp) cream in a piping bag. Spread the remainder over the meringues, top with fruit and decorate with a swirl of cream.

345 Calories per portion

Strawberry Pavlova SERVES 6

Egg whites - *3 (size 3)*
Caster sugar - *175g (6oz)*
Cornflour - *5ml (1 tsp)*
Vinegar - *5ml (1 tsp)*
Cornflour - *25g (1oz)*
Caster sugar - *25g (1oz)*

Fresh milk - *150ml (¼ pint)*
Brandy - *15ml (1 tbsp)*
Fresh whipping cream - *150ml (5 fl oz) lightly whipped*
Fresh strawberries - *225g (8oz)*
Baby meringues - *to decorate*

METHOD

1 Draw a 18cm (7 inch) circle on a sheet of non-stick paper. Place, pencil side down, on a baking sheet.

2 Whisk the egg whites until stiff. Whisk in 75g (3oz) sugar, then carefully fold in the remaining sugar, cornflour and vinegar with a metal spoon.

3 Spread the meringue over the circle and bake at 170°C (325°F), mark 3 for 1 hour.

4 Blend cornflour and 25g (1oz) sugar with 45ml (3 tbsp) milk in a saucepan. Gradually blend in the remaining milk and heat gently, stirring continuously until the mixture thickens and boils. Cool then stir in the brandy and whipped cream. Spread over the pavlova and decorate with strawberries and baby meringues.

---

430 Calories per portion

Orange Flummery with Strawberries

SERVES 6

Fresh double cream - *450ml (15 fl oz)*
Fresh milk - *300ml (½ pint)*
Sugar - *50g (2oz)*
Gelatine - *15ml (1 tbsp)*
Orange - *1, grated rind and juice*
Rosewater - *15ml (1 tbsp) optional*
Fresh strawberries - *225g (8oz)*
Orange slices - *to decorate*

METHOD

1 Heat the cream, milk and sugar until very hot but not boiling.

2 Sprinkle gelatine over the orange juice in a cup. Stand cup in a pan of simmering water and stir until gelatine has dissolved.

3 Stir gelatine into the cream followed by the orange rind and rosewater (if used). Pour into 6 wetted moulds and chill until set. Turn out and serve with strawberries and orange slices.

275 Calories per portion

Orange & Strawberry Chantilly SERVES 6

Oranges - *3 large*
Fresh strawberries - *350g (12oz)*
Brandy - *30-45ml (2-3 tbsp)*
Fresh whipping cream - *300ml (½ pint)*
Icing sugar - *40g (1½ oz) sifted*
Egg white* - *1 (size 3)*
*See page 2

METHOD

1 Put the oranges in a bowl, cover with boiling water and leave for 10 minutes. (This makes the skin and pith easier to remove.)

2 Drain oranges, remove peel and pith. Chill.

3 Halve strawberries and place in a serving dish. Thinly slice the oranges, arrange over the strawberries and sprinkle with brandy. Chill for at least 1 hour.

4 Whip the cream until softly stiff, stir in the sifted icing sugar and stiffly beaten egg white. Pile over the fruit and serve immediately.

130 Calories per portion

Coeur à la Crème SERVES 4

Cottage cheese - *225g (8oz)*
Caster sugar - *25g (1oz)*
Fresh double cream - *30ml (2 tbsp)*
Egg whites* - *2 (size 3)*
Fresh strawberries or raspberries - *to serve*
*See page 2

METHOD

1 Sieve cottage cheese into a basin and blend in the sugar and cream.

2 Whisk egg whites until stiff and gently fold into the cottage cheese with a metal spoon. Spoon into individual dishes, smooth the surface and chill. Serve with fresh fruit.

305 Calories per portion

Chestnut Dessert   SERVES 4

Fresh whipping cream - *150ml (5 fl oz)*
**Canned sweetened
    chestnut purée** - *225g (8oz)*
Greek style yogurt - *40g (8 tsp) to serve*

METHOD

1 Whip the cream until softly stiff.
2 Gradually fold into the chestnut purée with a metal spoon.
3 Pile or pipe into individual dishes and chill for 1 hour.
4 Spoon over a little yogurt before serving.

360 Calories per portion

New Year's Cheesecake   SERVES 10

Cottage cheese - *450g (1lb) sieved*
Lemons - *2, grated rind and juice*
Gelatine - *11g sachet*
Eggs* - *2 (size 3), separated*
Caster sugar - *75g (3oz)*
Fresh whipping cream - *300ml (½ pint)*
Digestive biscuits - *175g (6oz) crushed*
Butter - *75g (3oz) melted*
*See page 2

METHOD

1 Brush a loose bottomed 20.5cm (8 inch) cake tin with oil.
2 Mix the cottage cheese, lemon rind and juice.
3 Sprinkle gelatine over 30ml (2 tbsp) hot water in a basin. Stand in a pan of simmering water and stir until gelatine dissolves.
4 Blend egg yolks with the sugar, stir into the gelatine and heat until the mixture thickens slightly. Cool, then add to the cottage cheese.
5 Whisk the egg whites until stiff. Whip the cream until softly stiff.

6 When the mixture is on the point of setting, fold in half the cream and the egg whites. Pour into the tin and chill.
7 Mix biscuits and melted butter. Press lightly onto the cheesecake. Chill. Turn out and decorate with the remaining cream.

Cold Desserts

370 Calories per portion Ⓕ

Pumpkin & Mincemeat Pie
SERVES 8

Shortcrust pastry - *made with 200g (7oz) flour*
Mincemeat - *60ml (4 tbsp)*
Canned pumpkin - *410g (14oz) can*
Soft light brown sugar - *100g (4oz)*
Cinnamon - *5ml (1 tsp)*

Ginger - *2.5ml (½ tsp)*
Salt - *2.5ml (½ tsp)*
Eggs - *2 (size 3), lightly beaten*
Fresh milk - *150ml (¼ pint)*
Fresh whipping cream - *150ml (5 fl oz), whipped*

METHOD

1 Line 23cm (9 inch) flan ring with the pastry. Spread with mincemeat.

2 Combine pumpkin, sugar, spices, salt, eggs and milk in a large bowl and mix well. Pour over the mincemeat.

3 Bake at 220°C (425°F), mark 7 for 15 minutes. Reduce heat to 180°C (350°F), mark 4 and cook a further 35-40 minutes or until a knife – inserted in the mixture – comes out cleanly. Cool and decorate with whipped cream before serving.

---

435 Calories per portion Ⓕ

Chocolate Brandy Roll
SERVES 6

Custard powder - *25g (1oz)*
Sugar - *15g (½ oz)*
Fresh milk - *300ml (½ pint)*
Plain chocolate - *100g (4oz)*
Chocolate chip cookies - *1 packet*

Brandy or rum - *45ml (3 tbsp)*
Fresh double cream - *150ml (5 fl oz) lightly whipped*
Orange - *1*
Plain chocolate - *to decorate*

METHOD

1 Make custard using custard powder, sugar and milk as directed on the packet. Pour into a basin.

2 Melt chocolate in a basin over a pan of hot water. Stir into the custard. Pour 15ml (1 tbsp) milk over the surface and chill.

3 Stir milk into the custard. Dip each biscuit quickly in the brandy. Sandwich together with the custard to form a roll. Chill for 2 hours.

4 Add the grated rind of half the orange to the cream and spread over the biscuit roll. Serve chilled, decorated with slices of orange and chocolate.

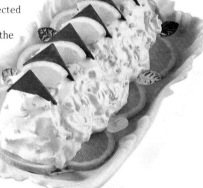

450 Calories per portion using whipping cream/480 Calories per portion using double cream.

Raspberry Amaretto Trifle SERVES 8

Trifle sponges - *1 packet*
Low sugar raspberry jam - *60ml (4 tbsp)*
Sherry - *150ml (¼ pint)*
Amaretto liqueur - *45ml (3 tbsp)*
Ground almonds - *100g (4oz)*
Ratafia biscuits - *50g (2oz) crumbled*

Fresh or drained canned raspberries - *225g (8oz)*
Egg yolks - *4 (size 3)*
Caster sugar - *40g (1½ oz)*
Cornflour - *15g (½ oz)*
Fresh milk - *450ml (¾ pint)*
Fresh whipping or double cream - *300ml (½ pint)*
Ratafia biscuits - *to decorate*

METHOD

1 Halve trifle sponges and sandwich together with jam. Cut into quarters and arrange in a trifle dish.

2 Pour sherry and 15ml (1 tbsp) liqueur over the sponges, sprinkle with 75g (3 oz) ground almonds and the ratafias. Reserving a few raspberries for decoration, place remainder in the dish.

3 Blend egg yolks, sugar and cornflour with a little milk. Heat remaining milk in a saucepan. When hot, blend in the cornflour and heat gently, stirring continuously, until thick.

4 Remove custard from the heat, stir in the remaining Amaretto, ground almonds and 45ml (3 tbsp) cream. Cool. Pour over the fruit, cover and chill.

5 Whip remaining cream until softly stiff. Place one third in a piping bag; spread the remainder over the custard. Decorate with swirls of cream, ratafias and raspberries.

---

315 Calories per portion Ⓕ

Green Goddess SERVES 6

Gelatine - *11g sachet*
Eggs* - *4 (size 3) separated*
Caster sugar - *50g (2oz)*
Fresh milk - *450ml (¾ pint)*
Crème de menthe - *30ml (2 tbsp)*
Fresh double cream - *150ml (5 fl oz) lightly whipped*
Finely chopped nuts and mints - *to decorate*
* See page 2

METHOD

1 Sprinkle gelatine over 30ml (2 tbsp) hot water in a cup. Stand in a pan of simmering water and stir until dissolved.

2 Beat yolks and sugar in a basin until pale yellow. Stir in boiling milk. Whisk over a pan of boiling water for 15 minutes until thick. Remove from the heat, add gelatine and cool.

3 Whisk the egg whites until stiff.

4 Fold the crème de menthe, half the cream, then a spoonful of egg white into the mixture with a metal spoon. Fold in remaining egg white. Pour into 6 ramekins or 500ml (1 pint) soufflé dish with paper collars. Chill for 4 hours. Remove collars and decorate with cream, nuts and mints.

245 Calories per portion Ⓕ

Mocha & Rum Soufflé

SERVES 6

Gelatine - *11g sachet*
Cocoa powder - *25g (1oz)*
Instant coffee granules - *5ml (1 tsp)*
Fresh milk - *450ml (¾ pint)*

Eggs* - *4 (size 3) separated*
Caster sugar - *75g (3oz)*
Rum - *30ml (2 tbsp)*
Fresh double cream - *150ml (5 fl oz) lightly whipped*
Chocolate curls - *to decorate*
*See page 2

METHOD

1 Sprinkle gelatine over 30ml (2 tbsp) hot water. Stand cup in a pan of simmering water. Stir until gelatine dissolves.

2 Whisk cocoa and coffee into the milk and bring to the boil.

3 Beat egg yolks and sugar in a basin until pale yellow. Gradually beat in the milk. Heat, while whisking, over a pan of hot water for 10-15 minutes until thick. Remove from the heat. Stir in the rum and gelatine. Allow to cool.

4 Whisk the egg whites until stiff.

5 Fold half the whipped cream, then a spoonful of egg white, into the custard mixture using a metal spoon. Fold in remaining egg white. Pour into a 500ml (1 pint) soufflé dish with a paper collar. Chill for 4 hours. Remove collar. Decorate with cream and chocolate.

---

255 Calories per portion

Black Cherry Maypole

SERVES 6

Black cherry jelly - *135g (4¾ oz) packet*
Canned pitted black cherries - *425g (15oz) can, drained*
Gelatine - *10ml (2 tsp)*
Fresh milk - *150ml (¼ pint)*
Curd cheese - *75g (3oz)*
Fresh double cream - *150ml (5 fl oz)*
Lemon juice - *15ml (1 tbsp)*

METHOD

1 Dissolve jelly in 300ml (½ pint) boiling water. Stir in 150ml (¼ pint) black cherry syrup and the black cherries. Leave in a cool place until slightly set.

2 Sprinkle gelatine over 15ml (1 tbsp) hot water in a basin. Stand over a pan of hot water, stirring until dissolved. Add milk and stir well. Beat into the curd cheese, add cream and lemon juice. Leave in a cool place until slightly set.

3 Layer the two mixtures in a wetted 1.1 litre (2 pint) deep ring mould. When set, turn out onto a serving plate. Place a chocolate flake or stick of rock in the centre and decorate with ribbons.

320 Calories per portion **F**

Christmas Trifle SERVES 6

Christmas pudding - *4 slices, approx 175g (6oz)*
Orange - *1, grated rind and juice*
Custard powder - *30ml (2 tbsp)*
Sugar - *25g (1oz)*
Fresh milk - *568ml (1 pint)*
Fresh whipping cream - *150ml (5 fl oz)*
Brandy - *15ml (1 tbsp)*
Flaked almonds - *25g (1oz) toasted – to decorate*

METHOD

1 Cut the pudding into pieces and arrange in a
trifle dish. Sprinkle with orange juice.

2 Blend custard powder, sugar and 30ml (2 tbsp)
milk. Heat remaining milk and pour onto custard
powder. Return to the pan. Heat, stirring
continuously until the custard thickens and boils. Cool.
Pour over the pudding.

3 Whip the cream until softly stiff. Stir in the
orange rind and brandy. Spread
over the custard.
Serve sprinkled
with almonds.

320 Calories per portion **F**

Ginger Pear Trifle SERVES 6

Fresh pears - *450g (1lb)*
Cider - *150ml (¼ pint)*
Soft brown sugar - *40g (1½ oz)*
Jamaica ginger cake - *½ cake, sliced*
Custard - *made with 300ml (½ pint) milk*
Fresh whipping cream - *150ml (5 fl oz)*
Flaked almonds - *25g (1oz) toasted*

METHOD

1 Simmer pears in a saucepan
with the cider and sugar until soft.

2 Place ginger cake in a trifle dish.
Spoon pears and juice over the top,
followed by the cooled custard.

3 Whip the cream until softly
stiff. Spread over the custard
and chill. Serve sprinkled
with toasted almonds.

500 *Calories per portion with full fat cheese* / 450 *calories per portion with curd cheese* **F**

Fresh Raspberry Cheesecake   SERVES 6

Digestive biscuits - *175g (6oz) crushed*
Butter - *75g (3oz)*
Fresh milk - *300ml (½ pint)*
Eggs* - *3 (size 3) separated*
Caster sugar - *50g (2oz)*

Gelatine - *11g sachet*
Full fat or curd cheese - *225g (8oz)*
Lemon juice - *15ml (1 tbsp)*
Lemon rind - *2.5ml (½ tsp)*
Fresh raspberries - *450g (1lb)*
*See page 2

METHOD

1 Grease a loose bottomed 18cm (7 inch) deep cake tin.

2 Stir biscuits into melted butter. Press into the base of the cake tin.

3 Place milk in a saucepan and pour in lightly beaten yolks. Heat, stirring continuously, until the sauce thickens. Do not boil. Remove from the heat, stir in the sugar.

4 Sprinkle gelatine over 30ml (2 tbsp) hot water in a cup. Stand in a pan of hot water, stirring until dissolved.

5 Place cheese in a bowl. Blend in the custard, lemon rind, juice and gelatine. Whisk until the mixture begins to thicken.

6 Fold a spoonful of stiffly whisked egg white into the custard with a metal spoon. Gently fold in the remaining egg white. Pour over the biscuit base and chill. Remove from the tin and serve decorated with raspberries.

---

435 *Calories per portion* **G**

Apple Cheesecake   SERVES 6

Digestive biscuits - *100g (4oz) crushed*
Butter - *50g (2oz)*
Eggs - *2 (size 3)*
Caster sugar - *75g (3oz)*
Full fat soft cheese - *225g (8oz)*
Cinnamon - *5ml (1 tsp)*
Apple purée - *150ml (¼ pint)*
Sultanas - *50g (2oz)*
Fresh soured cream - *150ml (5 fl oz)*
Fresh milk - *150ml (¼ pint)*
Dessert apple - *1 sliced, to decorate*
Lemon juice - *for dipping apple slices*

METHOD

1 Stir biscuits into melted butter. Press into the base of a loose bottomed 20.5cm (8 inch) cake tin.

2 Beat eggs and sugar until thick and creamy. Gradually beat in the soft cheese, then cinnamon, apple purée, sultanas, soured cream and milk. Pour over the biscuits.

3 Bake at 180°C (350°F), mark 4 for 1¼ hours. Turn oven off. Leave to cool in the oven. Remove from the tin and decorate with apple slices.

415 Calories per portion Ⓕ

Apricot Iceberg Slice SERVES 6

Digestive biscuits - *100g (4oz) crushed*
Butter - *50g (2oz) melted*
Fresh single cream - *150ml (5 fl oz)*
Fresh double cream - *150ml (5 fl oz)*
Icing sugar - *25g (1oz) sifted*
Ground almonds - *25g (1oz)*
Canned apricot halves - *425g (15oz) can, drained*

Eggs whites* - *2 (size 3) whisked*
Blanched almonds and chocolate - *to decorate*
*See page 2.

METHOD

1 Lightly grease a 1kg (2.2lb) loaf tin. Line with a double strip of foil, the width of the tin and long enough to overlap at the ends.

2 Stir biscuits into the melted butter and press on top of the foil in the base.

3 Whip the creams with the sugar until softly stiff.

4 Using a metal spoon, fold the ground almonds, followed by half the apricots (finely chopped) and the whisked egg whites into the cream. Pour into a loaf tin, smooth the surface and freeze until firm.

5 Use the foil 'ends' to lift the dessert from the tin. Place on a serving dish and decorate with remaining apricots, chocolate coated almonds and extra whipped cream, if desired.

---

140 Calories per portion

Iced Blackcurrant Creams SERVES 6

Custard powder - *15ml (1 tbsp)*
Sugar - *15ml (1 tbsp)*
Fresh milk - *300ml (½ pint) + 15ml (1 tbsp)*
Egg whites* - *3 (size 3)*
Canned blackcurrant pie filling - *400g (14oz) can*
Fresh whipping cream - *45ml (3 tbsp) for decoration*
*See page 2

METHOD

1 Using custard powder, sugar and milk, make up custard as directed on the tin. Pour 15ml (1 tbsp) milk onto the surface and leave to cool. Stir in the milk when ready to use.

2 Whisk the egg whites until stiff, fold into the custard with a metal spoon and pour into a 1 litre (1¾ pint) container suitable for the freezer. Freeze until the mixture has begun to freeze round the edge.

3 Remove from the freezer, beat well and fold in most of the pie filling. Return to the freezer and leave until frozen.

4 Serve in individual dishes, topped with the remaining pie filling and a swirl of whipped cream.

235 *Calories per portion*

Marshmallow Ice Cream

SERVES 6

Pink marshmallows - *100g (4oz)*
Fresh milk - *150ml (¼ pint)*
Eggs* - *2 (size 3)*
Icing sugar - *25g (1oz)*
Vanilla essence - *5ml (1tsp)*
Fresh double cream - *150ml (5 fl oz), lightly whipped*

*See page 2

METHOD

1 If you have one, switch on the 'fast freeze' setting on your freezer, one hour before you start – the quicker the mixture freezes, the better the texture of the ice cream.

2 Cut marshmallows in half. Place in a saucepan with the milk and heat gently until melted.

3 Whisk the eggs, icing sugar and vanilla essence. Stir in the marshmallow mixture, then the lightly whipped cream.

4 Pour into a freezer container. Freeze until the ice cream has frozen 1cm (½ inch) around the edges. Turn into a chilled bowl, break up with a fork then stir until smooth.

5 Return to a clean, dry container and freeze for 1½-2 hours or until firm. Transfer to the refrigerator for about 30 minutes to soften, before serving.

425 *Calories per portion*

Last Minute Christmas Pudding

SERVES 6

Plain cake or biscuit crumbs - *225g (8oz)*
Mixed dried fruit - *100g (4oz)*
Glacé cherries - *75g (3oz) chopped*
Nuts - *50g (2oz) chopped*
Thick custard - *300ml (½ pint)*

Apricot jam - *45-60ml (3-4 tbsp) melted*
Brandy or sherry - *15-30ml (1-2 tbsp)*
Fresh double cream - *150ml (5 fl oz) lightly whipped*
Fresh single cream or fromage frais - *to decorate*

METHOD

1 Mix all ingredients well, folding the lightly whipped cream in last of all.

2 Spoon into a 1 litre (1¾ pint) basin. Freeze until firm.

3 Dip basin briefly in hot water to remove the pudding. Serve with cream or fromage frais.

480 Calories per portion

Marquise Alice

SERVES 8

Egg yolks - *4 (size 3)*
Caster sugar - *150g (5oz)*
Pinch of arrowroot
Fresh milk - *300ml (½ pint) warmed*
Gelatine - *11g sachet*

Sherry - *15ml (1 tbsp)*
Peanut brittle - *100g (4oz) crushed*
Fresh whipping cream - *300ml (10 fl oz) whipped*
Chocolate finger biscuits - *2 packets*
Raspberry jam - *15ml (1 tbsp) sieved*

METHOD

1 Mix the egg yolks, sugar and arrowroot in a bowl. Stir in the milk and return to a heavy based saucepan. Cook gently, stirring continuously, until the custard just coats the back of a spoon.

2 Sprinkle the gelatine over 45ml (3 tbsp) hot water in a basin over a pan of simmering water. Stir until dissolved.

3 Pour gelatine into the hot custard, add the sherry and peanut brittle and chill until just beginning to set. Fold in half the whipped cream.

4 Line the base of a 15cm (6 inch) loose bottomed cake tin with greased greaseproof paper. Arrange the fingers around the edge of the tin. Put 5 in the base. Spoon in the custard. Chill until set.

5 Remove from the tin, top with the remaining cream and decorate with jam.

---

410 Calories per portion

Cherry Meringue Gateau

SERVES 8

Egg whites - *5 (size 3)*
Caster sugar - *275g (10 oz) + 15ml (1 tbsp)*
Custard powder - *30ml (2 tbsp)*
Fresh milk - *300ml (½ pint)*
Fresh whipping cream - *300ml (10 fl oz) lightly whipped*
Cherry pie filling - *385g (14oz) can*
Cherry brandy - *15ml (1 tbsp)*
Flaked almonds - *25g (1oz) toasted*

METHOD

1 Whisk the egg whites until stiff. Gradually whisk in 275g (10 oz) caster sugar. Spoon into a piping bag fitted with a large star nozzle.

2 Line two baking sheets with parchment. Pipe a 23cm (9 inch) diameter base on one and a decorative border, the same diameter, on the other. Bake at 110°C (225°F), mark ¼ for 3 hours. Peel off the parchment.

3 Prepare custard using the custard powder, milk and remaining sugar as directed on the packet.

4 Fold half the whipped cream into the custard and spread over the meringue base. Pipe the remaining cream around the edge. Place the meringue ring on top.

5 Mix the pie filling with the cherry brandy, pile into the centre and decorate with flaked almonds.

Cold Desserts

150 Calories per portion

Irish Coffee SERVES 1

Sugar - *5ml (1 tsp)*
Irish whiskey - *15ml (1 tbsp)*
Strong black coffee - *60ml (4 tbsp)*
Fresh double cream - *15ml (1 tbsp)*

METHOD

1 Place sugar in a warmed glass. Add whiskey, then hot coffee and stir well.

2 Place a teaspoon, face down, so it rests on the edge of the glass with the tip just touching the coffee. Carefully pour the cream over the back of the spoon so that it floats on the surface. Sip the coffee through the cream.

355 Calories per portion

Cider Syllabub SERVES 6

Cider - *90ml (6 tbsp)*
Caster sugar - *75g (3oz)*
Lemon - *1, finely grated rind and juice*
Fresh double cream - *300ml (10 fl oz)*
Shortbread - *6 biscuits, to serve*

METHOD

1 Combine cider, sugar, lemon juice and rind in a bowl. Leave to stand for at least 2 hours.

2 Add the cream and whisk until the mixture stands in soft peaks.

3 Spoon into glass dishes. Chill for several hours. Serve with shortbread.

350 Calories per portion

Autumn Apple Shortbread SERVES 6

Butter - *100g (4oz)*
Caster sugar - *50g (2oz)*
Plain flour - *175g (6oz)*
Apricot jam - *15ml (1 tbsp)*
Bramley cooking apples - *450g (1lb) stewed*
Sultanas - *30ml (2 tbsp)*
Currants - *30ml (2 tbsp)*
Orange - *1, finely grated rind and juice*
Whipped cream - *to decorate*

METHOD

1 Cream the butter and sugar until light and fluffy. Using a fork, gradually blend in the flour. Draw mixture together with fingertips, wrap in foil and chill for 30 minutes.

2 Divide shortbread in half and press each into a 18cm (7 inch) sandwich tin. Bake at 190°C (375°F), mark 5 for 15-20 minutes. Cool for 5 minutes, mark one into 6 portions and leave in tins to cool.

3 Spread base layer with jam. Mix the remaining ingredients and spread over the base. Position shortbread portions on top and decorate with cream.

Cakes

355 Calories per slice **F**

Spiced Apple Cake MAKES 12 SLICES

Self raising flour - *350g (12oz)*
Mixed spice - *10ml (2 tsp)*
Butter - *175g (6oz)*
Soft brown sugar - *175g (6oz)*
Sultanas - *225g (8oz)*
Egg - *1 (size 3) beaten*
Fresh milk - *200ml (7 fl oz)*

Bramley cooking apples -
    2 medium, cored and sliced
Demerara sugar - *25g (1oz)*
Clear honey - *to glaze*

METHOD

1 Lightly grease and line a 20.5cm (8 inch) deep cake tin.

2 Sift the flour and spice. Rub in the butter until the mixture resembles fine breadcrumbs. Add the sugar and sultanas. Blend beaten egg and milk, add to the dry ingredients and mix to a soft consistency.

3 Place half the mixture into the cake tin, cover with half the apples then the remaining mixture. Decorate with the remaining apples and sprinkle with demerara.

4 Bake at 190°C (375°F), mark 5 for 1¾ hours or until golden. Cover with foil during baking, if the apples are over browning.

5 Cool in the tin for 15 minutes, then turn onto a wire rack to cool completely. Remove lining paper and glaze with warmed honey.

---

200 Calories per portion **F**

Streusel Cake MAKES 16 SLICES

Butter - *100g (4oz) softened*
Caster sugar - *175g (6oz)*
Eggs - *1 (size 3)*
Fresh milk - *150ml (¼ pint)*
Self raising flour - *225g (8oz)*
Soft brown sugar - *75g (3oz)*
Cinnamon - *5ml (1 tsp)*
Walnut pieces - *50g (2oz) chopped*

METHOD

1 Cream 75g (3oz) butter and the caster sugar until light and fluffy. Beat in the egg and milk and carefully fold in 200g (7oz) flour.

2 Rub together the remaining butter, flour, brown sugar and cinnamon. Add the walnuts.

3 Spread half the cake mixture in a greased 28 x 18cm (11 x 7 inch) cake tin. Sprinkle with half the nut mixture, top with remaining cake mixture then the remaining nut mixture.

4 Bake at 180°C (350°F), mark 4 for 35-40 minutes. Cut into 16 slices while warm.

Cakes

230 Calories per slice ⓕ

Farmhouse Fruit Cake

MAKES 20 SLICES

Plain flour - *225g (8oz)*
Mixed spice - *10ml (2 tsp)*
Bicarbonate of soda - *5ml (1 tsp)*
Wholemeal flour - *225g (8oz)*
Butter - *175g (6oz)*
Soft brown sugar - *225g (8oz)*
Mixed dried fruit - *225g (8oz)*

Egg - *1 (size 3) beaten*
Fresh milk - *300ml (½ pint) approx*
Cubes of sugar - *5*

METHOD

1 Sift the plain flour, spice and soda into a bowl. Stir in the wholemeal flour.

2 Rub in the butter until the mixture resembles fine breadcrumbs. Stir in the sugar and fruit.

3 Make a well in the centre and add the beaten egg and enough milk to give a dropping consistency. Turn into a greased and base lined 20.5cm (8 inch) square tin. Scatter crushed sugar cubes over the top.

4 Bake at 170°C (325°F), mark 3 for 1 hour 40 minutes or until an inserted skewer comes out cleanly. Cool on a wire rack before serving.

---

390 Calories per slice ⓕ

Boiled Fruit Cake

MAKES 12 SLICES

Mixed dried fruit - *350g (12oz)*
Glacé cherries - *150g (5oz)*
Dried mixed peel - *50g (2oz)*
Walnut pieces - *50g (2oz)*
Soft brown sugar - *175g (6oz)*
Butter - *100g (4oz)*
Mixed spice - *5ml (1tsp)*

Bicarbonate of soda - *2.5ml (½ tsp)*
Fresh milk - *300ml (½ pint)*
Self raising flour - *350g (12oz) sifted*
Eggs - *2 (size 3)*

METHOD

1 Line a 20.5cm (8 inch) deep cake tin with greased greaseproof paper. Wrap the outside with brown paper.

2 Put the dried fruit, cherries, mixed peel, walnuts, sugar, butter, spice, bicarbonate of soda and milk into a saucepan. Bring to the boil and simmer for 5 minutes.

3 Cool to blood heat and stir in the flour and eggs.

4 Turn mixture into the tin. Bake at 170°C (325°F), mark 3 for 40 minutes, then reduce to 150°C (300°F), mark 2 and bake for 1½ hours.

5 Cool in the tin for 5 minutes, turn onto a wire rack, remove paper and leave until cold. Store in an airtight tin.

Chocolate Fudge Cake

570 Calories per portion

SERVES 12

Butter - *175g (6oz) softened*
Caster sugar - *175g (6oz)*
Eggs - *3 (size 3) beaten*
Cocoa powder - *30ml (2 tbsp)*
Self raising flour - *250g (9oz) sifted*
Fresh milk - *200ml (7 fl oz)*

ICING
Fresh double cream - *175ml (6 fl oz)*
Icing sugar - *450g (1lb) sifted*
Salt - *pinch*
Plain chocolate - *75g (3oz) grated*
Butter - *40g (1½ oz)*
Whipped cream and chocolate - *to decorate*

METHOD

1 Cream butter and sugar until light and fluffy. Gradually beat the eggs, then stir in the cocoa – dissolved in a little hot water. Add the flour, alternating with the milk. Beat until smooth.

2 Place in a 20.5cm (8 inch) lightly greased heart shaped tin. Bake at 180°C (350°F), mark 4 for 1 hour or until firm. Cool slightly, then turn onto a wire rack to cool completely.

3 Bring cream to the boil in a saucepan. Remove from the heat, add the sugar, salt and chocolate. Heat, stirring, until the chocolate melts. Cover and cook for 3 minutes without stirring. Uncover, reduce the heat to low and cook until the mixture reaches 115°C (240°F) or until a teaspoon of mixture, dropped into iced water, forms a soft ball.

4 Remove the pan from the heat. Cool in cold water until the base of the pan is cold. Beat in the butter until the icing is of a spreading consistency.

5 Sandwich the cake together with some of the icing. Cover the top and sides with the rest. Decorate with cream and chocolate.

Chocolate Marble Cake

355 Calories per slice **F**

MAKES 12 SLICES

Butter - *225g (8oz) softened*
Caster sugar - *225g (8oz)*
Eggs - *3 (size 3)*
Self raising flour - *350g (12oz)*
Salt - *pinch*
Fresh milk - *200ml (7 fl oz)*
Cocoa powder - *25g (1oz)*

METHOD

1 Cream the butter and sugar. Add the eggs, one at a time, beating well. Fold in the flour, salt and milk.

2 Divide the mixture between two bowls. Fold cocoa into one, mixing well.

3 Spoon the mixtures alternatively into a greased 20.5cm (8 inch) deep cake tin, to give a "marble" effect.

4 Bake at 170°C (325°F), mark 3 for 1½ hours until well risen. Cool and turn out on a wire rack. Store in an airtight tin.

Cakes

Hazelnut Torte

SERVES 8

Eggs - *2 (size 3)*
Caster sugar - *150g (5oz)*
Hazelnuts - *100g (4oz) ground*
Fresh whipping cream - *175ml (7½ fl oz)*
Butter - *50g (2oz)*

Fresh milk - *60ml (4 tbsp)*
Cocoa powder - *50g (2oz)*
Vanilla essence - *2.5ml (½ tsp)*
Icing sugar - *225g (8oz)*
Whole hazelnuts and crystallised violets - *to decorate*

METHOD

1 Grease and base line two 15cm (6 inch) sandwich tins.

2 Whisk the eggs and caster sugar until light and fluffy. Fold in the ground hazelnuts. Divide between the tins and bake at 200°C (400°F), mark 6 for 15 minutes until golden brown. Cool before removing from the tins.

3 Whip the cream until softly stiff. Use just over half to sandwich the tortes.

4 Place the butter and milk in a saucepan. Heat until boiling. Whisk in the cocoa and simmer for 30 seconds. Remove from the heat, stir in the vanilla essence and gradually beat in the icing sugar.

5 Spread icing over the torte and decorate with the remaining cream, hazelnuts and crystallised violets.

---

405 Calories per portion

Easter Bonnet Cake

SERVES 12

Self raising flour - *135g (4½ oz)*
Cocoa powder - *40g (1½ oz)*
Butter - *175g (6oz) softened*
Caster sugar - *175g (6oz)*
Eggs - *3 (size 3)*
Fresh milk - *60ml (4 tbsp)*
Fresh whipping cream - *75ml (2½ fl oz)*
Icing sugar - *450g (1lb) sifted*
Peppermint essence - *few drops*
Green food colouring - *optional*
Crystallised flowers - *to decorate*

METHOD

1 Sift flour and cocoa together.

2 Cream butter and sugar until light and fluffy. Beat in the eggs, one at a time, adding 15ml (1 tbsp) flour with each one. Fold in the milk and remaining flour with a metal spoon.

3 Turn into two greased and base lined 18cm (7 inch) sandwich tins. Bake at 180°C (350°F), mark 4 for 25-30 minutes until firm. Leave in the tins for 2-3 minutes then turn onto a wire rack to cool.

4 Sandwich cakes together with whipped cream.

5 Put icing sugar in a bowl. Gradually add approximately 60ml (4 tbsp) hot water, stirring briskly until the icing is smooth and coats the back of a spoon without running off. Add peppermint essence to taste and enough food colouring to give pale green icing.

6 Place the cake on a board, cover with icing and leave to set. Decorate with ribbon and crystallised flowers.

160 Calories each

Cherry Mallow Bars

MAKES 16

Digestive biscuits - *100g (4oz) crushed*
Butter - *50g (2oz)*
Marshmallows - *225g (8oz)*
Fresh milk - *150ml (¼ pint)*
Gelatine - *10ml (2 tsp)*
Chocolate digestive biscuits - *150g (5oz) crushed*
Glacé cherries - *50g (2oz) quartered*

METHOD

1 Stir digestives into melted butter. Press into a greased 18cm (7 inch) square tin. Chill.

2 Warm marshmallows in milk in a bowl over a pan of simmering water for 15 minutes. Stir frequently until melted. Chill for 30 minutes.

3 Sprinkle gelatine over 20ml (4 tsp) hot water in a bowl over a pan of hot water. Stir until dissolved.

4 Fold chocolate biscuits and cherries into the marshmallow mixture. Stir in the gelatine. Spoon over the biscuit base. Chill until set, then cut into bars.

685 Calories each

Coconut Castles

MAKES 6

Butter - *100g (4oz) softened*
Caster sugar - *100g (4oz)*
Eggs - *2 (size 3), beaten*
Self raising flour - *100g (4oz)*
Lemon juice - *30ml (2 tbsp)*
Creamed coconut - *½ 200g (7oz) packet, softened*
Fresh double cream - *150ml (5 fl oz)*
Icing sugar - *325g (11oz) sifted*
Red food colouring - *few drops*
Whipped cream and crystallised rose petals - *to decorate*

METHOD

1 Cream the butter and sugar until light and fluffy. Gradually beat in the eggs with a little flour. Fold in remaining flour.

2 Fill 6 dariole moulds, no more than two thirds full, with the mixture. Bake on a baking sheet at 180°C (350°F), mark 4 for 20 minutes or until golden. Cool on a wire rack.

3 Blend the lemon juice into the creamed coconut. Stand for 30 minutes. Blend in the cream and sugar. Liquidise until smooth and tint pale pink with food colouring. Chill if not firm enough to spread.

4 Level the bases of the cakes and coat with icing. Chill until set. Decorate with whipped cream and crystallised petals.

120 Calories per unbuttered slice **F**

Orange Teabread

MAKES 12 SLICES

Self raising flour - *225g (8oz)*
Salt - *large pinch*
Caster sugar - *15ml (1 tbsp)*
Butter - *50g (2oz)*
Chopped mixed peel - *25g (1oz)*
Orange - *1, grated rind only*
Fresh milk - *150ml (¼ pint)*

METHOD

1 Mix flour, salt and sugar in a bowl. Rub in the butter until the mixture resembles fine breadcrumbs. Stir in the mixed peel and orange rind.

2 Add sufficient milk to mix to a soft dough.

3 Knead lightly on a floured board and turn into a well greased 450g (1lb) loaf tin. Brush lightly with milk. Bake at 200°C (400°F), mark 6 for 35-40 minutes or until golden. Cool and serve lightly spread with butter.

190 Calories per unbuttered slice **F**

Ginger Cake

MAKES 12 SLICES

Plain flour - *225g (8oz)*
Ground ginger - *15g (½ oz)*
Baking powder - *5ml (1 tsp)*
Nutmeg - *large pinch*
Butter - *100g (4oz)*
Caster sugar - *100g (4 oz)*
Egg - *1 (size 2) separated*
Fresh milk - *75ml (5 tbsp)*
Butter for spreading

METHOD

1 Sift the flour, ginger, baking powder and nutmeg into a bowl.

2 Cream the butter and sugar until light and fluffy. Beat in the egg yolk. Then fold in the flour and milk.

3 Whisk the egg white until frothy and fold into the mixture. Pour into a greased 20.5cm (8 inch) cake tin. Bake at 180°C (350°F), mark 4 for 45 minutes until pale and firm. Cool on a wire rack before serving.

50 Calories per scone Ⓕ

Drop Scones

MAKES 24

Self raising flour - *225g (8oz)*
Salt - *2.5ml (½ tsp)*
Caster sugar - *15ml (1 tbsp)*
Egg - *1 (size 3)*
Fresh milk - *300ml (½ pint)*
Butter - *melted for brushing the pan*
Jam, honey or golden syrup - *to serve*

METHOD

1 Sift flour and salt into a bowl. Add sugar and mix to a smooth batter with the egg and half the milk. Add remaining milk. Do this as quickly and lightly as possible. Do not beat.

2 Brush a hot, heavy based frying pan lightly with butter. Drop spoonfuls of batter into the pan. Cook until bubbles show on the surface (about 2-3 minutes). Turn over and cook for 2 minutes more.

3 Pile scones into a clean, folded tea towel to keep warm and moist. Serve immediately with jam, honey or syrup.

70 Calories per scone Ⓕ

Apple & Raisin Drop Scones

MAKES 24

Plain flour - *225g (8oz)*
Bicarbonate of soda - *5ml (1 tsp)*
Cream of tartar - *5ml (1 tsp)*
Pinch of salt
Sugar - *50g (2oz)*
Eggs - *2 (size 3) beaten*
Fresh milk - *300ml (½ pint)*

Raisins - *25g (1oz)*
Dessert apples - *225g (8oz) cored and sliced*
Glacé cherries - *12, halved*
Golden syrup and whipped cream - *to serve*

METHOD

1 Sift flour, bicarbonate of soda, cream of tartar and salt into a bowl. Add sugar and gradually mix in the eggs and milk to give a smooth batter. Add the raisins.

2 Place apple rings, ½cm (¼ inch) thick, on a greased griddle or heated frying pan. Put half a cherry in each.

3 Cover apple rings with a spoonful of batter. Cook until bubbles show on the surface. Turn over and cook for 2 minutes more. Keep warm and moist in a clean tea towel. Serve with whipped cream and warmed syrup.

Scones & Biscuits

165 Calories per scone Ⓕ

Apple & Cinnamon Scones MAKES 10

Bramley cooking apples - *350g (12oz) cored and chopped*
Sugar - *25g (1oz)*
Self raising flour - *225g (8oz)*
Salt - *2.5ml (½ tsp)*
Ground cinnamon - *5ml (1 tsp)*
Butter - *50g (2oz)*
Fresh milk - *150ml (¼ pint)*

Demerara sugar - *25g (1oz)*
Whipped cream - *to serve*

METHOD

1 Cook apples with sugar and a little water until soft. Mash well and cool.

2 Sift flour, salt and cinnamon into a bowl. Rub in the butter until the mixture resembles fine breadcrumbs.

3 Make a well in the centre, add one third of the apple and the milk. Mix to a soft dough.

4 Knead lightly and roll out to 1.5cm (¾ inch) thick. Cut into 10 rounds – 5cm (2 inch) thick.

5 Place on a greased baking sheet, brush with milk and sprinkle with demerara. Bake towards the top of the oven at 230°C (450°F), mark 8 for 10-15 minutes or until golden. Cool.

6 Serve filled with remaining apple and whipped cream.

---

240 Calories per portion Ⓕ

St. George's Scone SERVES 6

Self raising flour - *175g (6oz)*
Baking powder - *5ml (1 tsp)*
Salt - *2.5ml (½ tsp)*
Mustard powder - *5ml (1 tsp)*
Pinch of cayenne pepper
Butter - *40g (1½ oz)*
English Cheddar cheese - *50g (2oz) grated*
Fresh milk - *125ml (4 fl oz)*
Leicester cheese - *50g (2oz)*

METHOD

1 Sift flour, baking powder, salt, mustard and cayenne into a bowl. Rub in the butter until the mixture resembles fine breadcrumbs. Stir in the grated cheese and milk. Mix to a soft dough.

2 Knead lightly and roll out to a circle about 1cm (½ inch) thick and 23cm (9 inch) in diameter. Place on a greased baking sheet.

3 Make a cross on the dough using strips of Leicester cheese 5cm (2 inch) wide. Brush the dough with milk.

4 Bake at 200°C (400°F), mark 6 for about 20-25 minutes or until risen and golden brown.

235 Calories per portion Ⓕ

Hot Cross Buns MAKES 12

Fresh yeast - *15g (½ oz)*
Sugar - *50g (2oz)* + ¼ tsp
Fresh milk - *225ml (8 fl oz) + 30ml (2 tbsp)*
Strong plain flour - *450g (1lb)*
Salt - *2.5ml (½ tsp)*
Mixed spice - *5ml (1 tsp)*
Ground cinnamon - *5ml (1 tsp)*

Eggs - *2 (size 3)*
Butter - *50g (2oz) melted*
Raisins - *50g (2oz)*
Chopped candied peel - *50g (2oz)*
Shortcrust pastry - *25g (1oz) optional*
Fresh milk and sugar - *to glaze*

METHOD

1 Crumble yeast into a bowl and blend in ¼ teaspoon sugar. Add 30ml (2 tbsp) luke warm milk and blend well. Leave in a warm place for 15-20 minutes.

2 Sift sugar, flour, salt and spices into a large bowl. Make a well in the centre and pour in the yeast mixture, remaining milk, eggs and butter. Draw the flour mixture into the liquid. Mix well.

3 Turn onto a floured board and knead for 10 minutes. Shape into a ball, place in a greased bowl, cover with a damp cloth and leave in a warm place for 1 hour or until doubled in size.

4 Turn onto a floured board, knead lightly, working in the raisins and peel. Cut into 12 pieces and shape into buns.

5 Arrange 5cm (2 inch) apart on a greased baking sheet and leave in a warm place until doubled in size.

6 Roll out pastry, cut into strips and make crosses on the buns. Brush with the milk/sugar mixture. Bake at 220°C (425°F), mark 7 for 20-25 minutes. Cool on a wire rack.

210 Calories per portion Ⓕ

Cheese Shortbread SERVES 8

Butter - *100g (4oz)*
Plain flour - *100g (4oz)*
Ground rice - *50g (2oz)*
English Cheddar cheese - *50g (2oz) finely grated*
Cayenne pepper and chopped parsley - *to garnish*

METHOD

1 Rub the butter into the flour and ground rice until the mixture resembles fine breadcrumbs.

2 Stir in the cheese and a pinch of cayenne.

3 Press into a 20.5cm (8 inch) sandwich tin or roll out and cut into shapes and arrange on a baking sheet.

4 Bake at 180°C (350°F), mark 4 for 30-40 minutes for the tin and 15-20 minutes for the shapes. Serve sprinkled with cayenne and parsley.

350 Calories per portion **F**

Gingerbread Men   MAKES 6

Self raising flour - *225g (8oz)*
Ground ginger - *10ml (2 tsp)*
Mixed spice - *2.5ml (½ tsp)*
Butter - *100g (4oz)*
Caster sugar - *75g (3oz)*
Black treacle - *30ml (2 tbsp) melted*
Fresh milk - *30ml (2 tbsp)*
Currants, angelica, glacé cherries - *to decorate*

METHOD

1 Sift the flour, ginger and spice into a bowl. Rub in the butter until the mixture resembles fine breadcrumbs. Stir in the sugar.

2 Add the melted treacle and milk and mix to a stiff paste.

3 Roll out thinly onto a floured surface and cut out gingerbread men using a shaped cutter. Place on a greased baking sheet and decorate with currants, angelica and cherries.

4 Bake at 180°C (350°F), mark 4 for 10 minutes until golden. Leave to cool for 3 minutes. Transfer to a wire cooling rack. Leave until cold.

80 Calories per portion **F**

Easter Biscuits   MAKES 30

Self raising flour - *225g (8oz)*
Salt - *pinch*
Butter - *150g (5oz)*
Caster or icing sugar - *100g (4oz) sifted*
Egg - *1 (size 3) approx.*

METHOD

1 Sift the flour and salt into a bowl. Rub in the butter until the mixture resembles fine breadcrumbs. Add sugar and sufficient beaten egg to give a very stiff dough.

2 Knead lightly on a floured board until smooth, wrap in foil and chill for 30 minutes.

3 Roll out fairly thinly then cut out 30 circles using a 5cm (2 inch) cutter.

4 Place biscuits on a greased baking sheet, prick well with a fork and bake at 180°C (350°F), mark 4 for 12-15 minutes, until pale gold.

5 Cool for 2-3 minutes then transfer to a wire rack. Store in an airtight tin when cold.

Sweets

1135 Calories per lb jar

Thick Orange Marmalade

MAKES 2.5kg (5lb)

Seville oranges - *700g (1½ lb)*
Lemon - *1, juice only*
Granulated or preserving sugar - *1.4kg (3lb)*
Butter - *15g (½ oz)*

METHOD

1 Scrub the oranges well, place in a large saucepan, pour in 1.7 litres (3 pints) water and bring to the boil.

2 Cover and simmer gently for 1½-2 hours or until the peel is soft and can be easily pierced with a fork.

3 Remove oranges from the pan. Cool slightly. Chop coarsely. Reserve the pips and tie in a muslin bag.

4 Return oranges and pips to the pan. Add lemon juice and sugar. Heat slowly, stirring all the time. When the sugar has dissolved, bring to the boil.

5 Boil rapidly for 15-20 minutes until setting point is reached.

6 Remove from the heat. Stir in butter to disperse the scum. Leave until a skin forms, stir gently, then pot.

30 Calories per portion

Chocolate Fudge

MAKES 80 PIECES

Granulated sugar - *450g (1lb)*
Fresh milk - *150ml (¼ pint)*
Butter - *50g (2oz)*
Chocolate - *50g (2oz) grated*

METHOD

1 Place the sugar and milk in a heavy saucepan. Leave to stand for 1 hour.

2 Add the butter and chocolate to the saucepan and heat gently, stirring all the time, until the sugar has dissolved. Bring to the boil and boil for 20-30 minutes until a little of the mixture forms a soft ball when dropped into a bowl of cold water.

3 Pour into a 20.5cm (8 inch) square greased tin and leave to set. Turn out and cut into pieces.

120 Calories per truffle

Chocolate Rum & Raisin Truffles MAKES 20

Dark rum - *30ml (2 tbsp)*
Raisins - *50g (2oz)*
Sponge cake - *100g (4oz) crumbled*
Digestive biscuits - *100g (4oz) crushed*
Ground almonds - *50g (2oz)*
Plain chocolate - *100g (4oz)*
Fresh double cream - *100ml (4 fl oz)*
Chocolate vermicelli and cocoa - *for coating*

METHOD

1 Soak the rum and raisins for a few hours or overnight.

2 Stir in the cake crumbs, biscuits and ground almonds.

3 Melt the chocolate in a basin over a pan of hot water. Stir in the cream and cake mixture. Chill well.

4 Form into balls and coat in vermicelli or cocoa.

Coconut Ice *45 Calories per piece*
MAKES 64 PIECES

Caster sugar - *450g (1lb)*   **Desiccated coconut** - *150g (5oz)*
Fresh milk - *150ml (¼ pint)*   **Red food colouring** - *few drops*

METHOD

1 Lightly grease a 20.5 x 15cm (8 x 6 inch) shallow tin.

2 Slowly dissolve the sugar in the milk. Bring to the boil. Boil gently for 10 minutes or until the mixture reaches 116°C (240°F) on a sugar thermometer. Remove from the heat. Add the coconut.

3 Spread half the mixture into the tin. Colour remainder pink and pour over the first layer. Cool, then mark into 2 x 2.5cm (1 x 1¾ inch) pieces. Cut when cold.

110 Calories per lolly

Eskimo Ices MAKES 6

Instant dessert mix - *300ml (½ pint) packet, any flavour*
Fresh milk - *300ml (½ pint)*
Sugar strands, vermicelli, chocolate - *to decorate*

METHOD

1 Make up the dessert with milk as directed on the packet.

2 Spoon into lolly moulds and freeze for several hours.

3 Remove from the moulds and dip in chocolate and sugar strands to decorate just before serving.

Each recipe serves 2

Milk Shakes

CHILLED CHOCOLATE SHAKE   *215 Calories per glass*
Blend together
Drinking chocolate – *20ml (4 tsp)* and
Boiling water – *30ml (2 tbsp)*
Whisk in
Chilled fresh milk – *400ml (⅔ pint)* and
Vanilla essence – *a few drops*
Serve topped with
Whipping cream – *15ml (1 tbsp), whipped* and
Grated chocolate – *5ml (1 tsp)*

TROPICAL FRUIT SHAKE   *210 Calories per glass*
Blend together
Banana – *1 medium, mashed* with
Orange juice – *30ml (2 tbsp)* and
Pineapple juice – *30ml (2 tbsp)*. Add
Fresh chilled milk – *300ml (½ pint)*
Place a scoop of
Vanilla Dairy Ice Cream in each glass.
Top with fruity milk and
Grated orange rind (optional).
Serve immediately.

RASPBERRY CRUSH   *200 Calories per glass*
Blend together
Raspberry purée – *75ml (5 tbsp)* and
Icing sugar – *10ml (2 tsp) sifted,* with
Chilled fresh milk – *300ml (½ pint)*
Whisk for a few seconds in a liquidiser.
Place a scoop of
Vanilla Dairy Ice Cream – in each glass.
Top with raspberry milk. Serve immediately.

Each recipe serves 2

Iced Cold Milk Drinks

MINT CUP   *155 Calories per glass*
Whisk together
Chilled fresh milk – *400ml (⅔ pint)* and
Peppermint essence – *a few drops* and
Icing sugar – *15ml (1 tbsp) sifted,* and
Green food colouring – *a few drops,* in a blender
for a few seconds until foamy
Serve immediately.

ICED COFFEE   *120 Calories per glass*
Fresh milk – *300ml (½ pint)* is added to
Double strength sweetened
Coffee – *300ml (½ pint)*
Serve chilled, topped with whipped cream (optional).

SUMMER FIZZ   *115 Calories per glass*
Chilled fresh milk – *200ml (⅓ pint)* and
Chilled lemonade – *200ml (⅓ pint)* and
Oranges – *juice of 2,* are whisked in a blender
until foamy.
Serve immediately.

YOGURT COOLER   *170 Calories per glass*
Whisk together
Chilled fresh milk – *300ml (½ pint)* and
Whole fruit yogurt – *150g (5oz)* in a blender
for a few seconds until foamy.
Serve immediately.

Drinks

Each recipe serves 2

Drinks for the Family

MARSHMALLOW FOAM   *195 Calories per glass*
Marshmallows – *6, roughly chopped, are heated* with
Fresh milk – *400ml (⅔ pint)*
Just as marshmallows begin to melt,
pour into cups. Serve sprinkled with
Cinnamon.

WHISKY AND HONEY WARMER   *190 Calories per glass*
Clear honey – *15ml (1 tbsp)* and
Whisky – *15ml (1 tbsp)* are stirred into
Fresh milk – *400ml (⅔ pint)*
Heat until the honey melts.
Serve immediately.

NANA-BERRY MILKSHAKE *245 Calories per glass*
Whisk together
Raspberry yogurt – *150g (5oz)* and
Banana – *1 peeled and mashed* and
Fresh milk – *400ml (⅔ pint)* in a blender
for a few seconds.
Serve immediately.

AFTER EIGHT MILK   *195 Calories per glass*
Whisk together
Drinking chocolate – *20ml (4 tsp)* and
Peppermint essence – *a few drops* and
Hot fresh milk – *400ml (⅔ pint)* in a blender
for a few seconds until foamy.
Reheat. Serve sprinkled with
Drinking chocolate powder or
Grated chocolate.

Each recipe serves 1 except Banana Banshee serves 2

Cocktails with Fresh Cream

BANANA BANSHEE   *165 Calories per glass*
Blend together
Banana – *1 small, mashed*
Vodka – *30ml (2 tbsp)*
Crème de caçao – *30ml (2 tbsp)*
Fresh double cream *30ml (2 tbsp)*
in a liquidiser for a few seconds.
Serve in glasses, sprinkled with brown sugar.

PINA COLADA COCKTAIL   *145 Calories per glass*
Blend together
White rum – *15ml (1 tbsp)*
Coconut liqueur – *15ml (1 tbsp)*
Pineapple juice – *15ml (1 tbsp)*
Fresh double cream – *15ml (1 tbsp)* with
Crushed ice in a liquidiser
until thick and frothy. Serve immediately.

BRANDY ALEXANDER   *135 Calories per glass*
Mix together
Brandy – *15ml (1 tbsp)*
Crème de Caçao – *15ml (1 tbsp)*
Fresh double cream – *15ml (1 tbsp)*
and shake well. Serve immediately.

GRASSHOPPER   *65 Calories per glass*
Fill a glass with
Crushed ice. Pour over
Crème de Menthe – *15ml (1 tbsp)* and top with
Fresh single cream – *15ml (1 tbsp)*
Serve immediately.

Index

Index

Index